A Century of Royal Children

INGRID SEWARD

First published in September 2013.
Second Edition November 2013.

Text copyright: Ingrid Seward
Pictures: Press Association Images;
TRH The Duke and Duchess of Cambridge (pages 18 and 19);
Private Collection (pages 38, 40, 43, 44, 50 and 51);
Joe Little (page 190);
Mark Stewart (pages 198, 201, 202 and 203).

Design copyright: Mpress (Media) Ltd
Editor: Joe Little

ISBN: 978- 0- 9572559- 9- 9

Published By:
Rex Publications Ltd
64 Charlotte Street
London W1T 4QD
Telephone: 020 7436 4006
www.majestymagazine.com

Designed and Printed by mpress
Unit Four, Ashton Gate, Harold Hill, Romford, RM3 8UF Tel: 01708 379777

Contents

Introduction

FAMILY LIFE HAS always been central to the British monarchy. It is what they are there for – to stand as a symbol of continuity, a regal bulwark against the decline of moral values and changing social mores.

As Prince Philip explained: 'If you are really going to have a monarchy, you have got to have a family, and the family has got to be in the public eye.' The monarchy has been very much in the public eye, and the family – the royal family – has become a national obsession.

More than the adult members of the royal family, it has always been the children, in all their burnished innocence, in all their ordinariness, who provide the symbolic hope for the future – of the royal family, and of the nation. From the moment of each royal child's birth, every detail of their development – no matter how mundane, how insignificant – has been recorded in gushing tones. The first tooth, the first step and the first word, all broadcast in tones of reverential excitement. The colour of the royal offspring's hair and eyes discussed, clothes studied and copied. Even the names of the nannies made front-page news.

But the foundations beneath the House of Windsor shift with the changing times and it is this ability to change at a measured pace that is one of its great strengths.

The family, once so regal, so secure, from time to time finds itself on the defensive, its role the subject of a fundamental reappraisal. As first one, then three, of the marriages of the Queen's children came to their ends, the methods by which they were raised – methods that seemed so right at the time – came to be widely regarded as a woefully inadequate training for dealing with the pressures of the modern age.

'Everyone has to have a sense of duty,' Prince Philip once observed. 'A duty to society, to their family. If you haven't got a sense of duty you get the sort of community we have now.'

Yet 'duty', in the all-consuming royal sense that puts the public performance before the needs of the individual, can exact its emotional toll. It did with Charles, Anne and Andrew – to the incomprehension of the Queen.

'And I thought I had brought them up so well,' Her Majesty remarked to Lord Charteris, her former private secretary, as she surveyed the marital ruptures in her children's lives in that '*annus horribilis*' of 1992. The Duke of York parted from his wife, Sarah; Princess Anne divorced and then remarried; and, most damaging of all, the Prince and Princess of Wales officially separated. In the end duty wasn't enough to hold the family together, and each announcement stripped away another layer of the mystique which George V believed was the royal family's greatest strength.

The King insisted that the dignity of their royal position had to be maintained at all times, and he carried this through into his family life. He summed up his attitude towards his offspring in a remark to the Earl of Derby: 'My father was frightened of his mother, I was frightened of my father, and I am damned well going to see that my children are frightened of me.'

He succeeded in his aim. His eldest son, David, later Duke of Windsor, wrote: 'We were, in fact, figuratively speaking, on parade, a fact that he would never allow us to forget.'

George V's children rarely saw him. When they did, they had to bow before they were allowed to speak. From the viewpoint of the early 21st century, their letters home to their stern, intolerant father make poignant, pathetic reading.

'You must learn to behave like a boy and not like a little child,' the King had written to ten-year-old son Henry, the future Duke of Gloucester, who dutifully, fearfully replied: 'Dear Papa, Thank you very much for the nice letter you so kindly sent me…'

OPPOSITE PAGE: The Queen, the Duke of Edinburgh and their four children on the eve of their Diamond Wedding anniversary, November 2007

George VI, mindful of the unhappiness of his childhood, tried to make amends with his daughters, even going to the extent of bathing them himself – an almost unheard-of indulgence at the time. On matters educational, however, the rule of benign neglect still applied. Elizabeth and Margaret's mother, the late Queen Mother, felt that the object of her daughters' education was to learn how to dance, draw, appreciate music and to acquire good manners and 'lots of pleasant memories stored up against the days that might come and, later, happy marriage'.

It was left to the future Queen Elizabeth II and her forthright husband to bring the family into line with the modern world. The royal family still dwelt in their palaces, surrounded by courtiers, but they started to assimilate the new and decidedly more affectionate approach to childcare developed in the United States. Children were no longer seen and not heard.

The art of being royal, as the Queen pointed out, was a matter of practice. 'Training is the answer to a great many things,' she said. 'You can do a lot if you are properly trained – and I hope I have been.'

Prince Charles agreed. 'I've learnt the way a monkey learns: by watching its parents,' he remarked.

As Diana, Princess of Wales once observed of her elder son, William: 'I always feel he will be all right because he was born to his royal role. He will get accustomed to it gradually.'

His relations can give him specific advice, such as 'never cancel an engagement; if you have a headache take an aspirin' (Prince Philip); 'never show emotion in public' (the Queen); and '*never* look at your feet' (the Queen Mother).

But if the deportment and decorum of royalty is there to be learnt by rote, there are other aspects that require more personal attention.

'What is much more difficult is bringing them up as people,' said Prince Philip. 'I've always tried to help them master at least one thing, because as soon as a child feels self-confidence in that area, it spills over into others.'

He and Elizabeth tried to take a more caring interest in the development of their progeny. Writing to her midwife, Sister Helen Rowe, from Balmoral seven weeks after the birth of Anne, Princess Elizabeth revealed her motherly side.

'Charles is getting fatter, as he has an enormous appetite and takes a great deal of exercise,' she wrote. 'He enjoyed the train journey far more than Anne, who wasn't too keen on the rattling to begin with.'

As part of their preparation for their royal role – a role that many had started to complain was in danger of becoming out of date, of losing its point – the Queen and Prince Philip invited a steering committee of educationalists to Buckingham Palace to discuss the best way of educating their children. It was a pointless exercise: Philip's mind was already made up.

Tiring of the deliberations, he forcefully declared that his education had been good enough for him, and what was good enough for him was good enough for his children. Charles and Anne would be sent away to school.

As well intentioned as it might have been, this insistence on 'normality' was never an easy objective for members of the royal family to achieve. They see their photographs in the newspapers almost every day. They observe the obsequious manner in which powerful people approach their parents. They are lavished with gifts.

'However hard you try, it's almost impossible to bring them up as ordinary children,' Prince Philip admitted.

Princes William and Harry, so their father insisted, were 'normal little boys'. Up to a point. When William got in an argument at school he threatened his adversary with his grandmother's soldiers. And after he was hit on the head with a golf club he wrote to a friend to report on his recovery and warned him to lock the letter away so that it would not fall into the wrong hands.

As Prince Charles observed, everything they did created 'an abnormal amount of attention'.

That, given the privileged position they enjoy, is inevitable. But the pressure the attention generates, as Princess Margaret once said, can be 'perfectly dreadful'. It has been exacerbated for the modern generation by the tide of unfavourable stories that engulfed the royal family in the Eighties and Nineties.

It was worse for Prince William and his younger brother, Prince Harry. There was no way, no matter how hard anyone tried, that they could be shielded from the catalogue of misfortunes that overwhelmed their parents. The tragic death of their mother in 1997, followed by the public investigations and inquests that lasted until 2008, only served to keep the traumatic memories alive.

'It is almost impossible to describe what it is like being a member of the royal family,' the late Prince William of Gloucester remarked. 'I suppose in essence it comes down to this: you can never be your real self. Just to know you are royal inhibits you. It wasn't that anyone ever said to me, "You are a royal prince and you must act like one." I simply knew that whether I liked it or not, I was automatically separated by my heritage from the rest of the world.'

'I think the younger members find the regimented side difficult,' the Queen has conceded.

'The children soon discover that it is much safer to unburden yourself to a member of the family than a friend,' Prince Philip once stressed. 'You see, you're never quite sure. A small indiscretion can lead to all sorts of difficulties.'

The old routines of royalty are hard to break, however, and the outward structure is still in place. The family still comes together – at Balmoral and Sandringham – for their traditional holidays. The footmen still wear livery. And the nannies continue to underpin the system. They may be more likely to be able to foil a potential kidnapper than wear a uniform, but they are still an essential part of royal life.

In the last hundred years royal children have been brought up not by their parents but by the spinster daughters of forestry workers and policemen. It is the working-class nannies, not the royal mothers, who have assumed responsibility for what child psychologist Penelope Leach calls the 'nurturing and loving' so essential to the emotional development of any child.

It is the nannies who have been responsible for making sure that the youngsters in their care learn how to sit still, to say 'please' and 'thank you', and to curtail any bad habits. Most have been dedicated women who provided their royal charges with all the affection they required. But however caring and competent they may have been, they could never completely compensate for the lack of parental affection.

Nor could they break the 'glass wall' that isolates and protects their charges from the rigours of the real world. In this closeted environment there has been little room for individuality – or for the tactile affection most 'ordinary' families take for granted. Royal children are taught how to behave in public. They are not taught how to deal with private problems. Instead of having to learn how to cope with emotional situations, they are able to retreat behind the protective panoply of their position.

When Prince Andrew met Koo Stark, for instance, the following day he decided to terminate his relationship with his previous girlfriend, Christina Parker, a dancer with the Royal Ballet. Overwhelmed by Koo but unwilling to come clean with Christina, he instructed the Buckingham Palace switchboard to stop putting through her telephone calls and he never spoke to her again – exactly as his great-uncle, the Duke of Windsor, had done when he ended his liaison with Freda Dudley Ward.

However efficient that way may be when dealing with dispensable emotional jetsam, it is no method for dealing with the difficulties of married life.

To marry happily into the immediate royal family – if one is not royal oneself – appeared to be an impossibility. Then Sophie Rhys-Jones, the daughter of a retired tyre salesman, married Prince Edward and 12 years later, in April 2011, Catherine Middleton married Prince William. She was the first girl with true working-class roots to marry a future king and in doing so bring the monarchy closer to the people.

The cult of the royal family, with its attendant cast of children, uncles and aunts and distant cousins, is a Victorian invention. It was a sturdy, self-confident era and Britain was the richest nation in the world with an ever-expanding empire that embraced a quarter of the globe. Such power cried out for its own mythology, and to help provide it the concept of the 'royal family', which would symbolise all the inherent strengths of a nation at the zenith of its might, was conceived.

This natural development, engendered by chauvinistic national pride, was readily seized upon by the public, by the politicians and by the monarchy itself.

It was a temporal deity that drew its strength, not from any divinity (that notion died on the block with Charles I), but from those stolid Victorian virtues of moral rectitude, thrift, good manners and decorum that it came to represent. That certain members of the family should tumble from such an exalted pedestal was only to be expected.

'Like all the best families, we have our share of eccentricities, of impetuous and wayward youngsters and of family disagreements,' the Queen has acknowledged.

Of greater remark, however, than the fact that some members of the royal family fail to live up to what is expected of them is that most of them have, repaying homage with duty, the trappings of their majesty with a commitment to hard work.

'If you have privilege, which in my case you were born with, you have no option,' Prince Michael of Kent explained. 'You can't have all the perks without pulling your weight. You can't have it without some kind of obligation.'

It is an obligation, a sense of responsibility that is bred into them – often at great personal cost, as we have now seen – from the day the guns sound to salute their birth. And it is a way of royal life that is changing substantially as the royal family faces up to the challenge of sustaining its existence for the next century of royal children.

The Duke and Duchess of Cambridge leave St Mary's Hospital on 23 July 2013 with their one-day-old son

Catherine & George

THE BIRTH OF His Royal Highness Prince George Alexander Louis of Cambridge has secured the continuity of the monarchy into the next century. The infant Prince, third in line to the throne, will eventually be the 43rd monarch since William the Conqueror.

Perhaps it was the full moon, or the thunderstorms that briefly broke the heatwave smothering the country for almost three weeks, but at around 5.30am on Monday 22 July the Duke and Duchess of Cambridge were spotted by a freelance photographer entering St Mary's Hospital in Paddington. He tweeted the news, but there had been so many false starts that few took much notice as the early morning unfolded.

Two hours later Kensington Palace confirmed that the Duchess was in the early stages of labour but would not say if she was overdue or not. It was the news the world's press had been waiting for, as outside the entrance to the private Lindo Wing was the biggest media circus in royal history. Some photographers had been there since the beginning of July and even members of the public had taken up temporary residence on benches or in tents.

Journalists referred to it the 'Great Kate Wait' and because nothing was happening they had been reduced to interviewing each other and any member of the public they could find. What they couldn't do was lose their coveted place behind the barriers.

At 4.24 that afternoon, the Duchess of Cambridge gave birth to an 8lb 6oz boy. According to astrologers, the infant was born 40 minutes before the Cancer star sign turned to Leo.

The official announcement was delayed for four hours to give the royal couple time to telephone the Queen, Prince Charles, Prince Harry and the Middleton family from their suite in the Lindo Wing, where Prince William was able to spend the night. Like Prince Charles with Diana before him, William remained at Kate's side throughout her 11-hour labour. The Windsor princes may sometimes appear arrogant and distant, but they relish the prospect of fatherhood as much as any man and long to be involved.

When the news was officially announced via Twitter and email wild cries of delight broke out from the crowds outside the Lindo Wing and Buckingham Palace. The world's most eagerly awaited tweet, from Clarence House, said: 'The Duchess of Cambridge was safely delivered of a son at 4.24pm.' More followed: 'The baby weighs 8lb 6oz' and 'Her Royal Highness and her child are doing very well and will remain in hospital overnight.'

Twenty minutes later, the huge crowd that had gathered outside the palace cheered as the official announcement was placed on an easel in the forecourt, as it had been when Prince William was born 31 years earlier. The Queen, out of sight near a window in the Chinese Dining Room, watched the excitement below. Her Majesty, rather like Queen Victoria when the future Edward VIII was born in 1894, now has three generations of kings in waiting.

The announcement was signed by four of the medical team headed by 69-year-old Marcus Setchell, the Queen's former surgeon-gynaecologist, who was assisted by consultant obstetrician Guy Thorpe-Beeston, paediatric specialist Dr Sunit Godambe and the Queen's own physician, John Cunningham.

Alan Farthing, the current royal surgeon-gynaecologist, was also part of the team who were assisted by several midwives, on duty in shifts around the clock as is normal practice for a delivery of such magnitude.

As congratulations poured in from around the globe, the famous fountains in Trafalgar Square were lit blue, while at the top of the iconic BT Tower a flashing message informed Londoners: 'It's a Boy!'

RIGHT: Catherine, aged three-and-a-half, enjoys a holiday in the Lake District

OPPOSITE PAGE: The Middleton girls with father Michael in Jordan, where they lived for two years

A family snapshot of the future royal consort at the tender age of five

The Canadian side of Niagara Falls was also blue for the night, as was Story Bridge in Brisbane, Australia.

The following afternoon the King's Troop Royal Horse Artillery fired a 41-gun salute in Green Park, while at the Tower of London they went one better with a 62-gun salute. And if this were not enough, the bells of Westminster Abbey pealed out 5,000 changes over a three-hour period.

Whilst London celebrated, both sets of grandparents visited the infant Prince and his proud parents. First up were Carole and Michael Middleton, who arrived and departed in a taxi, followed later by the Prince of Wales and the Duchess of Cornwall, who had been helicoptered from official duties in Yorkshire. After a hesitant start Carole Middleton spoke briefly to the press about her 'beautiful' grandson.

At 7.13pm William and Kate, cradling their sleeping son, stepped on to those now familiar steps of the Lindo Wing.

William, who charmingly addressed his wife as 'Poppet', seemed genuinely happy to speak to the media throng. He admitted he had been watching them all waiting outside on television and told reporters that the baby had 'a good pair of lungs' and was 'a big boy – quite heavy'. He also confirmed that his son was born after his due date – joking that he would remind him of that when he was older.

Kate revealed how 'special and emotional' the experience was and – to her surprise – that William had already expertly changed his first nappy. The midwives made him do it, the Prince later explained.

The couple then briefly returned to the hospital before re-emerging with their son safely strapped into the baby car seat for the short drive home to Kensington Palace.

A historic meeting took place the following morning when the Queen visited her first great-grandson at Kensington Palace. It was 120 years since a reigning monarch had met a future king three generations ahead, when in 1894 Queen Victoria was introduced to the baby who would briefly become Edward VIII.

That evening Kensington Palace issued a further statement: 'The Duke and Duchess of Cambridge are delighted to announce that they have named their son George Alexander Louis. The baby will be known as His Royal Highness Prince George of Cambridge.'

There has only been one Prince George of Cambridge before, a military man with a racy love of life, born in 1819 and commemorated with a statue in Whitehall, where he is mounted on a fine horse. George is the regnal name of six of the nine Hanoverian/Windsor kings, the most recent being William's great-grandfather, George VI.

The last Prince George in the royal family was the Queen's uncle, the flamboyant and handsome Prince George, Duke of Kent, father of the present Duke of Kent, Prince Michael of Kent and Princess Alexandra. The late Duke was known within his family as 'Georgie' and Prince Charles remarked that this is how his grandson would most likely be known before long.

Louis is a reference to the late Earl Mountbatten of Burma, while Alexander is apparently a name the royal couple liked.

As William and Kate drove through leafy Berkshire lanes to the Middletons' new home at Bucklebury, the Duchess must have felt overwhelmed. Even Diana did not have quite so much fuss made when William was born and she was cosseted in her Kensington Palace apartment with staff to cook and clean and nannies to help with baby William round the clock. But the Manor House is a perfect secluded retreat and baby George became the first Prince – third in the line of succession – not to spend his first weeks in a royal palace. It bodes well for the modern world he will one day inherit and allowed Prince William, on two weeks' paternity leave, to bond with his son without the distractions of royal duties or royal staff.

Modern though they might be, the couple will still abide by royal tradition. Their London headquarters is the late Princess Margaret's sizeable Kensington Palace apartment, with its impressive walled garden, and they will also have the use of Anmer Hall in Norfolk as a country house.

Prince George will be educated at the best schools, probably including Eton College like his father, followed by university and then the armed forces. The crown he will eventually inherit will, however, be symbolic of a very different age where women are filling the most important roles. But if Prince George's firstborn child is a son, the United Kingdom will play host to more than a century of kings.

In a televised interview recorded two weeks after George's birth, William described the 'high' that he and his wife experienced on becoming parents.

'We were happy to show him off to whoever wanted to see him,' he revealed. 'As any new parent knows, you're only too happy to show off your new child and, you know, proclaim that he is the best looking or the best everything.'

William described his young son as a 'little bit of a rascal' and a 'fighter' who 'doesn't want to go to sleep that much'. He praised Kate for doing a 'fantastic job'.

He described it as an 'emotional' time and one that left him more affected than he ever thought he would be. But he couldn't resist joking about the sleepless nights and endless dirty nappies.

Asked about the legacy he would like to leave to his son, William quipped: 'At the moment, the only legacy I want to pass on to him is to sleep more and maybe not to have to change his nappy so many times.'

When Catherine Elizabeth Middleton was born in the Royal Berkshire Hospital in Reading on 9 January 1982, the idea she might one day produce a king for the 22nd century would have been laughable. Her parents, Michael and Carole, were an ordinary couple working hard to make a better life for themselves and their children.

Kate's maternal grandmother, Dorothy Goldsmith, who was born on a council estate, was the instigator and installed a sense of ambition in her two children – Carole and younger brother Gary – which motivated them all.

Dorothy was satisfied that she had done her job well as a mother when at the age of 21 Carole began working as an air hostess for what later became British Airways, which is where she met her future husband, aircraft dispatcher Michael Middleton, the second of four brothers from Leeds.

RIGHT: As the baby Prince sleeps, his proud parents acknowledge the cheers of the crowd gathered outside the Lindo Wing to see them leave

The Cambridges introduce their son to the massed ranks of the world's media and speak to reporters

OPPOSITE PAGE: A look of joy on the face of new mother Kate as she cradles her precious bundle

They married in June 1980 and bought their first home, a redbrick semi-detached house in the Berkshire village of Bradfield. When Catherine – Kate to her friends – was born in January 1982 Carole had already given up work; she gave birth to a second daughter, Philippa, in September 1983.

Apart from a brief sojourn living in Jordan, where Michael continued his job for British Airways, the family enjoyed a magical childhood in rural Berkshire. The Middletons were exceptionally close and did everything together, celebrating all the landmark events in their lives with a series of cleverly-themed parties.

They loved fancy dress and when recalling her best party ever, Kate chose to highlight 'the amazing white rabbit marshmallow cake that Mummy made for me when I was seven'.

Around the time Kate's brother James was born in 1987, Carole Middleton started what would eventually become a hugely successful online family business – Party Pieces. What followed were financial security and the opportunities that money provides.

This enabled Kate and Pippa to attend St Andrew's private prep school, near Pangbourne in Berkshire, where the future Duchess was the perfect pupil: joining the choir, taking the leading role in school plays and winning sports prizes. But Kate's written work wasn't quite so good, and the history master later recalled her failing to learn the dates of all the Kings and Queens of England.

Doing everything possible to give their children the best opportunities, Carole and Michael Middleton decided the next step for their sporty elder daughter would be the smart all-girls school, Downe House, near their new home in Bucklebury. It was not a success as instead of boarding the sweet-natured Kate was one of a few day pupils and was bullied for being a 'goody-goody'.

After two terms she was removed and enrolled in the prestigious co-educational Marlborough College, where mother Carole usually secured the prize for the biggest picnic on sports day – something the Princess of Wales went to great lengths to avoid when William and Harry were at Ludgrove.

Kate was as popular at Marlborough as she had been unpopular at Downe House and once she was enrolled in the all-girls residence, Elmhurst, she blossomed. Fellow pupils remember her as 'always sweet and lovely – she always did the right thing and was very, very sporty'.

Although Kate denied it when questioned in her engagement interview, she did have pictures of the teenage Prince William on her study wall. But their meeting was still years away and first Kate had to complete her education, pass her exams and get a place at a university of her choice. And she had the traditional middle-class post-school adventure to complete: a gap year.

In retrospect, everything Kate did was a subconscious learning curve for her to achieve the seemingly unachievable. Her charm, her poise, her dedication, her looks, her ability to talk to anyone, were the perfect training for a royal princess, except at 19 – when she met Prince William at St Andrews University – Kate had no idea that is what she would become. But she did, simply by being herself and being in the right place at the right time.

The Middleton family's part in Prince George's upbringing will be just as important as William's royal family. Carole's success in raising such a kind-hearted girl as Kate encourages us all to have faith that the dimension she will bring to her grandson's life will be both loving and essential.

ABOVE: Just like any father, the Duke of Cambridge carries George to the car in his baby seat

OPPOSITE PAGE: William, second in line to the throne, holds his newborn heir

William and Kate pose with their son for a portrait taken by grandfather Michael at the Middletons' home in Berkshire in early August 2013

OPPOSITE PAGE: The Cambridges and three-month-old George before his christening at the Chapel Royal, St James's Palace, 23 October 2013

Princess Elizabeth waves to the crowd as she and Clara Knight leave 145 Piccadilly in a carriage, May 1928

Elizabeth

ELIZABETH WAS NOT brought up to be Queen, nor was she brought up to shoulder responsibility, or get a job. She was brought up simply to enjoy a childhood that, as her governess observed, would provide her 'with lots of pleasant memories stored up against the days that might come and, later, happy marriage'.

The rigours of the three Rs were of secondary importance. Her mother had been taught to read the Bible and little else: it had been sufficient for her and it was expected to be enough for her daughter and, later, her younger child, Margaret.

'I often had the feeling,' the governess, Marion Crawford, recorded, 'that the Duke and Duchess, most happy in their own married life, were not over concerned with the higher education of their daughters.'

There was no apparent need for it, at least in their infancy. Elizabeth's father, Bertie, Duke of York, a second son, was a shy, unsure, frail man who was not destined for the throne and harboured no ambitions in that direction. He was a country man who had little interest in society, and was more than happy to let the sun of majesty shine on the blond head of his charismatic elder brother, David.

His wife was a woman of singular determination and great spirit, as events would prove. But in 1926, when their daughter made her entrance by Caesarean section at 2.40am on 21 April, the horizon of parental ambition extended no further than the comfortable expectations of their class and time.

Named Elizabeth Alexandra Mary – after her mother, great-grandmother and grandmother – she was the third grandchild and first granddaughter of George V and Queen Mary. The first General Strike in British history was only four weeks away, the barricades were being erected and there was talk of revolution.

But such social upheavals made little impact on the secure world – country houses and shooting parties and very occasional visits to Buckingham Palace – into which the young Princess was born. Her life was mapped out for her: a 'happy childhood'

followed by a suitable marriage to a European princeling, or more probably, since the King had changed the ruling that members of his family could only marry royalty, a member of the aristocracy; then children of her own. Her royal connection was a fact of blood, not of responsibility.

The baby Elizabeth was third in line to the throne – after her uncle and her father – but only, it was presumed, for the time being, until David married and had children of his own, or until her parents produced a son. And when that happened – and in 1926 everyone believed 'when' was an inevitability – Elizabeth would slip hardly observed down the line of succession into upper-class obscurity.

To ensure that the little Princess grew up into a young lady, Clara Knight, who in turn had been nanny to both the Duchess of York and her brother, David – and later to their elder sister Lady Elphinstone's children – was re-employed. She was a no-nonsense Hertfordshire woman who organised her young charge according to the same strict methods she had employed with the previous generation. Fashions in childrearing may change in most circles, but the routine of the old-fashioned English nanny does not.

Known as 'Allah' – a childish derivation of her Christian name – she had unchallenged control of the nursery. She subscribed to the view that it was harmful to pamper children. Everything – feeding, baths – had its time, and if the child chose to raise a cry of protest she was left to get on with it.

The Duchess raised no objections to such methods and allowed Allah to do her job in her own way. She had no reason to wish it otherwise. Elizabeth Bowes Lyon and all her family had been brought up in exactly the same way. The era of 'bonding' and the associated belief in the importance of a mother's tactile love were several generations away in the future. In the homes of the well-to-do, children were seen only twice a day, once in the morning and then again before they went to bed at night.

The Princess was no less loved for that. The Duchess of York – she was 25 when her elder daughter was born – was an adoring mother. The Duke, constrained by his own childhood, always found it difficult to show affection.

He found it embarrassing, Marion Crawford remembered, when his infant daughter, Margaret, wound her arms round his neck, nestled against him and cuddled and caressed him: 'He was not a demonstrative man.' But he did enjoy the sense of warm familial comfort his daughter's presence generated: he enjoyed bath-time and pillow fights and taught her how to play hopscotch.

Allah, too, despite all her sternness (another Bowes Lyon nanny remembers her as 'quite easy-going', but given the constraints of the time the term is comparative) was very fond of her ward. Elizabeth, when apprised of the unpleasant and sometimes violent misery a succession of unsuitable nannies had made of her father's childhood, would later be grateful for such fondness.

However much affection may have been showered on her, Elizabeth was still deemed only of secondary importance in the grand scheme of things, and when she was only nine months old her parents left her for an extended six-month tour of Australia.

How attitudes towards a mother's responsibilities have changed. When the Duchess left her baby for six months in 1927 she was applauded for doing her wifely duty. When the next Duchess of York left her newborn child, Beatrice, for less than six weeks in 1988 to travel to Australia to see her husband, she was subjected to an outburst of public disapprobation from which she never recovered.

But in 1927 it would have been deemed strange, if not downright disloyal, had the Duchess allowed her royal husband to undertake such an arduous trip alone.

It was the beginning of what for Elizabeth was going to have to be duty's lifelong victory over emotion, though, baby that she was, she was too young to remember the sound of those first salvos being fired. Hers was still a world of the most primal needs, and those were well taken care of, for as well as Nanny Allah, she also enjoyed the attentions of 22-year-old Margaret MacDonald – Elizabeth renamed her 'Bobo' – who was in charge of the nursery kitchen, and her 14-year-old sister, Ruby, who acted as under-nurse.

Elizabeth had been born at 17 Bruton Street in Mayfair, the London home of her maternal grandfather, the 14th Earl of Strathmore, whose ancestor had acquired the family's title by marrying the daughter of Scotland's king, Robert II. With her parents gone, it was decided to remove the bairn and her nursery entourage to Strathmore's 18th-century mansion at St Paul's Walden Bury in Hertfordshire, where Allah had started work for the Bowes Lyons in 1901 at the age of 17. The house was little used at that time, and a bitterly cold winter forced a tactical withdrawal the following month to London. They returned not to Bruton Street but to a speedily-organised nursery at Buckingham Palace, arriving on 10 February.

'Our sweet little grandchild arrived here yesterday and came to see us after tea,' George V recorded in his diary.

The King did not get on well with children of the male gender. His own sons had walked in fear of his louring temperament, and so did his grandsons, as one of them, George Lascelles, the future Earl of Harewood, remembered well. 'The possibility of getting something wrong was, where grandfather was concerned, raised to the heights of extreme probability, and our visits to Windsor for Easter usually provided their quota of uneasy moments.'

Even a child's occasional ill-health elicited no sympathy from the King-Emperor. One April, the then eight-year-old George Lascelles started to sneeze, 'either from the pollinated grass or sheer nerves, and no amount of assurance that I had hay fever could stop the shout of "Get that damn child away from me", which made a rather strong impression on an awakening imagination.'

The King, so unbending, so demanding with his male progeny, was more considerate towards the females. He had allowed his daughter Mary, whom he made Princess Royal, a licence he always denied her four brothers. And he doted, albeit in a gruff and frequently intimidating manner, on his eldest granddaughter. It was affection hard won. Neither Elizabeth nor her younger sister ever called him 'Grandpa England', as popular legend had it.

As Princess Margaret would later recall: 'We were much too frightened of him to call him anything but Grandpapa.'

Elizabeth, however, always appeared to have his measure. He called her 'Lilibet', the nickname given her by her sister Margaret when she was too young to pronounce Elizabeth. She would play with his beard – it tickled – and the Archbishop of Canterbury, Dr Cosmo Gordon Lang, once observed her tugging him along by it across the floor, on his hands and knees.

There was another side to this grandparental equation, which came in the form of Queen Mary, his imperious wife. If the King could occasionally let, if not his hair, then his beard down, she was always as ramrod-straight in manner as her back was to look at. A visit to this stiff, imposing woman, Princess Margaret would remember, brought a 'hollow, empty feeling to the pit of one's stomach'.

RIGHT: Composed from an early age, Princess Elizabeth and her younger sister, Margaret Rose, pose for a photograph in 1933

OPPOSITE PAGE: The Duke and Duchess of York with the sleeping baby Elizabeth on 29 April 1926, a week after her birth

The Princess has fun riding her tricycle in Hamilton Gardens while a friend tries to keep up

OPPOSITE PAGE: Elizabeth accompanies her uncle David, then Prince of Wales, to the Braemar Gathering in 1932

In a world where appearances counted for everything, Queen Mary had a mania for maintaining them. She had to, or so she thought, for this most royal of queens wasn't royal at all by the strict dictates of blood; or at least wasn't royal enough to be considered as the equal in rank to her British relations.

Queen Mary's grandfather, Duke Alexander of Württemberg, had ventured beyond his caste and married a Hungarian countess without a royal bloodline. Because their union was a morganatic one, Francis, their son – Queen Mary's father – was not allowed to succeed to the Württemberg throne. Queen Victoria, who was grand enough to make her own dynastic rules, wrote, 'I have always thought and do think it very wrong and very absurd that because his mother was not a princess he is not to succeed in Württemberg'.

Francis was allowed to marry Victoria's first cousin, Princess Mary Adelaide of Cambridge, who, like the Queen herself, was a granddaughter of George III.

This minor German princeling – who had been compensated for the loss of his inheritance with the title Prince Teck – encountered little competition for the hand of Mary Adelaide. She was exceedingly large and, as the Foreign Secretary, Lord Clarendon, drolly remarked, 'Alas, no German prince will venture on *so vast an undertaking*.' Good-looking Francis had no such reservations, for as well as having no throne he had no money, and being married to a princess, even one whose own lady-in-waiting felt moved to describe as looking like a 'large plush purple pincushion', did have its compensations.

Their daughter Mary – who was born in May 1867, the year after her parents' marriage, and thus nicknamed May by her mother, who called her 'my May-flower' – was never anything more than a poor relation, however, and one who was getting poorer. Her parents were profligate with what little money they had and the lot they borrowed, and when their daughter was 16 years old they were, as May observed, in Short Street. With creditors closing in and threatening writs, they debunked to Florence, where they remained for two years.

This background, coupled with her dubious pedigree, did not make her an enticing marriage prospect.

But again Queen Victoria intervened, and determined to marry her off. First she thought of one of her grandsons, Albert Victor, Duke of Clarence, notorious because of his rumoured involvement in the Jack the Ripper case and the Cleveland Street Scandal, which followed a police raid on a homosexual brothel. Then, when he died, she thought of his altogether more suitable brother, the future George V.

'So it came about,' Kenneth Rose wrote in his definitive biography *George V*, 'that a young woman without a fortune, seemingly condemned to spinsterhood by a flawed pedigree, found herself destined to be Queen Consort of Great Britain. In that sense Princess May was indeed a Cinderella, and Queen Victoria a godmother of unbounded benevolence.'

The humiliations suffered in childhood, however, were to govern the rest of her life. They would have a profound influence on the royal family, with effects which still echo to this day.

Mary – well educated, naturally intelligent and far more cultured than her husband – had developed a learned interest in the history of art during her enforced stay in Italy. Those attributes, however, were well concealed. Her friend, Mabell, Countess of Airlie, said of her: 'As a girl she had been shy and reserved, but now her shyness had so crystallised... The hard crust of inhibition which gradually closed over her, hiding the warmth and tenderness of her own personality, was already starting to form.'

The royal family have never been adept at welcoming outsiders into their regal nest, and Mary was treated with ill-disguised contempt by her sisters-in-law. Princess Louise, disdainful of her morganatic lineage, would loudly say: 'Poor May! Poor May! With her Württemberg hands.' Princess Victoria once ordered a guest at Windsor: 'Now do try to talk to May at dinner, though one knows she is deadly dull.' It is no wonder that this excruciatingly shy woman retreated into herself.

With her position as protection, she became oversensitive to the nuances of protocol and status, unwilling and eventually unable to soften the defensive persona of intimidating formality in which she swathed herself. She subjugated herself to her old-fashioned husband's will; the King did not approve of change, and Mary spent her life dressed in the styles of the Edwardian age he favoured – and expected her children to do the same.

'King George V and Queen Mary have often been depicted as stern, unloving parents, but this they most certainly were not,' Mabell, Countess of Airlie wrote.

'I believe that they were more conscientious and more truly devoted to their children than the majority of parents in that era. The tragedy was that neither had any understanding of a child's mind.' Age would soften her only imperceptibly; the self-enforced habits of a lifetime are hard to change.

This, then, was the old lady into whose effective control the Duchess entrusted her young daughter during her six-month absence, and under whose orders Allah now came.

In any disagreement with the Duchess, Allah had the right of reply. The Queen, however, had to be obeyed without question. The Duchess, in her dealings with her former nanny, was by childish habit still a child, and Allah the surrogate mother. In the presence of the formidable May of Teck, however, the usually formidable Allah reverted to being a servant highly regarded, one whose judgement and opinion were valued, but a servant nonetheless.

'Teach that child not to fidget!' the nanny was repeatedly commanded.

On the Queen's firm instructions, Elizabeth was taught to wave to the crowds on command, to pose for photographers, to control her bladder in return for the reward of a biscuit. To ensure that she didn't fidget, the pockets of her dress were sewn up. All this before she was three years old.

The Duchess herself was a part of this system. Many women run into difficulties with their mothers-in-law. For a young woman obliged by protocol to open and close any conversation with her husband's mother from the humbling position of a formal curtsey, a certain tension was inevitable. The Duchess may have harboured misgivings and resentments about the situation – it would have been unusual if she hadn't – but this was one cross-generational battle the former Elizabeth Bowes Lyon was not going to win.

Duty, as Queen Mary impressed upon her daughter-in-law, had always to come before personal considerations. The 'family firm', as Bertie called it, had a business to run.

The Duchess, whose own childhood had been a happy and united one, was distressed by the separation and took leave of her baby in floods of tears. As George VI's official biographer, Sir John Wheeler-Bennett, noted, the car that took the Yorks to the station to catch the train to Portsmouth where they embarked on the battle cruiser HMS *Renown* 'had to be driven around until she was composed enough to face the crowds'.

The Duchess had reason to be upset. By being away for those six months during that formative period, by allowing her own nursery staff to fall under the direct order of the most 'royal' of the 20th century's most formidable and caste-conscious royals, the Duchess had undermined her own maternal importance.

Queen Mary had no desire to usurp the mother's role; unless the King happened to be in the room when Elizabeth was brought into her sitting room after tea, the visit would only last a few minutes before she was whisked back to the nursery. Displays of affection were not Queen Mary's style. Smothering order and system was, and the reference point had been established.

When the Duchess eventually returned, the baby, who had thwarted Allah's efforts to get her to say 'Mother' or even 'Mama' (though she was quite able to say 'Allah' and 'Bobo'), refused to go into her arms.

There were tears and much hanging on to Nanny's skirts before Lilibet could be persuaded to join her mother for the requisite appearance on the Buckingham Palace balcony.

Putting that upsetting scene behind her, the Duchess determined to build a happy home of her own for her husband and her daughter. The Yorks moved out of Bruton Street and into 145 Piccadilly, where the InterContinental Hotel now stands. 'It might have been the home of any moderately well-to-do young couple starting married life,' Marion Crawford opined, with understatement.

It was more than that: an imposing four-storey mansion situated at the genteel heart of an empire's capital, with views from the back over the private Hamilton Gardens to Hyde Park and, from the front, across Green Park to Buckingham Palace. Elizabeth's nursery was on the top floor, 'comfortable, sunny rooms that opened on to a landing beneath a big dome'.

But it was a self-contained world edged with loneliness. Elizabeth had no one to play with other than her cousins, and they were rare visitors. The birth of her sister, Margaret Rose, on 21 August 1930, gave her a companion; but she was four years her junior and hardly a ready-made playmate.

'I shall call her Bud,' Lilibet declared.

'Why Bud?' Lady Cynthia Asquith enquired.

'Well, she's not a rose yet, is she? She's only a bud,' the elder Princess is said to have replied.

The Duke of York, giving unconscious expression to their isolation, referred to his family as 'us four'. The greater world was locked out, and Elizabeth and Margaret rarely mixed with other children. On their walks through Hyde Park they would see others of their age laughing and playing together, but they did not join in.

'Other children always had an enormous fascination, like mystic beings from a different world, and the little girls used to smile shyly at those they liked the look of,' Marion Crawford recalled. 'They would have loved to speak to them and make friends, but this was never encouraged. I often have thought it a pity. They seldom had other children to tea.'

Destined, as it turned out, for society's pinnacle, they were always outside society.

Margaret and Elizabeth are among the young guests at the Master of Carnegie's (centre) sixth-birthday party at Elsick House in Kincardineshire, September 1935

Elizabeth's real friends were not people. They were the foot-high toy horses on wheels that she collected. Eventually there were some 30 of them, each with its own saddle and bridle, and they were carefully stabled around the dome on the landing. Before she went to bed, Elizabeth would unsaddle them, to groom and water them. It was a 'must-be-done' chore every night.

In the early Thirties two books were published which allowed an unprecedented insight into the home life of members of the royal family. One was entitled *The Story of Princess Elizabeth*, written by Anne Ring, a former secretary to the Duchess. The other was Lady Cynthia Asquith's *The Married Life of Her Royal Highness The Duchess of York*; both were written with the 'personal approval of Her Royal Highness', both painted a cosy

picture of domestic bliss: of bath nights with the Duke (itself an unusual occurrence in an age where fathers rarely ventured on to the nursery floor), with Allah begging him 'not to get Lilibet too excited'; of Elizabeth and Margaret Rose armed with red brushes and dustpans 'with which every morning the little Princesses sweep the thick pile carpet'.

But if it was cosy it was also strictly ordered, with little room for individual expression or the inquisitive vagaries of infancy.

Elizabeth got up at 7.30am, breakfasted in the nursery, then joined her parents for 15 minutes before starting her lessons – a ritual that would continue right up to the morning of her wedding day.

At 11 o'clock she broke for half-an-hour for a biscuit and a glass of orangeade. Lunch was at 1.15pm, which, when she was a little older, she ate with her parents if they were at home. The afternoons were spent out of doors or, if it was raining, drawing, attempting to master knitting, which she was always very poor at, and studying music. Tea was at 4.45pm. Between 5.30pm and 6.30pm her mother came to play. Supper followed.

Then, punctually at 7.15pm, she was sent to bed. It was an inflexible routine broken only by trips to Scotland in the autumn and weekends spent at Royal Lodge, the Yorks' home in Windsor Great Park.

Marion Crawford arrived at 145 Piccadilly when Elizabeth was five years old. 'Until I came she had never been allowed to get dirty,' she remembered. 'Life had consisted of drives in the park, or quiet ladylike games in Hamilton Gardens, keeping to the paths; or leisurely drives around London in an open carriage, waving graciously to people when Allah told her to do so.'

Relations between Marion Crawford and Allah started off on the cool side. The nanny regarded her rival for the children's affection with a mixture of what the new governess called 'reserve and apprehension'.

The girls, perceptive as children are to moods, will have caught that initial atmosphere, though the two women eventually effected a stand-off of expedience. 'If on her side the neutrality was sometimes armed to the teeth, I was always very careful not to tread on her toes,' the governess recorded.

Marion Crawford, dubbed 'Crawfie' by Elizabeth, was a 22-year-old school teacher from Kilmarnock in Scotland who had worked with poor, undernourished, underdeveloped children in the slums of Edinburgh and, 'fired with a crusading spirit', had aspirations to become a child psychologist. Instead, a holiday job with the Earl and Countess of Elgin led to an

introduction to Lady Rose Leveson-Gower and then to her sister, the Duchess of York. She was offered a position. The Duchess, determined to have her own way at least in her own home, insisted upon having a young governess, and after a month's probationary trial, Crawford gave up her ambition to work with the deprived and accepted the post in one of the most privileged households in the country.

It was, she recalled, a very ordered household, though – despite its royal master – an unpretentious one. She introduced her charges to games of Red Indians and hide-and-seek, and allowed Elizabeth, to her great delight, to get herself dirty (but only when Allah wasn't looking). But the high point of what in retrospect seems their rather dull routine was watching the brewer's dray drawn by two horses, which passed by every day and drew up at the traffic lights below the nursery.

'The little girls, their faces pressed to the nursery window, would watch for them fondly, anxious if they were late,' Crawfie said. 'And many a weary little pony trotting home at the end of the day in its coster's cart little dreamed of the wealth of royal sympathy it roused from that upper window…

'No two children had a simpler outlook on life. Early to bed and very few treats or outings, and those of an extremely unsophisticated nature.' A trip on a double-decker bus, sitting upstairs of course, one journey by Underground to the YWCA at Tottenham Court Road, trips to Woolworth's to do their Christmas shopping, and one pantomime a year was the sum of their visits to 'the outside world of which they knew so little'.

Elizabeth was taught to ride and to fox hunt (her father wanted her 'blooded' with the Pytchley at the age of five but the fox got away that day), to swim, and to stalk stags in the Scottish Highlands. They were the kind of skills deemed necessary for well-born countrywomen. While they certainly did the young Elizabeth no measurable harm – she was, her governess remarked, always an 'immensely interesting child' with a high IQ – it was hardly an upbringing designed to broaden her intellectual or social viewpoint.

But that was not what was wanted. 'It was generally conceded in those days that the education of two not very important little girls did not matter a great deal,' Crawfie observed.

LEFT: Princess Elizabeth takes Dookie for a walk in Hyde Park in the spring of 1936, which came to be known as the 'year of three kings'

OPPOSITE PAGE: On her tenth birthday, 21 April 1936, Elizabeth goes for a ride on her new pony in Windsor Great Park

King George V's only instruction to his granddaughters' governess was to make sure they learned how to write properly. 'I like a hand with some character in it,' he decreed.

The indomitable Queen Mary, on the other hand, had the most decided views on the education of the next generation of a dynasty that was not hers in name but was half hers by morganatic bloodline.

Crawfie had been in trepidation of her first meeting with the imperious May of Teck, and had spent the morning practising her curtsey before the oak tree in Hamilton Gardens. (Trees provide invaluable royal training. The last Kaiser's grandmother was the only member of the Prussian court who did not find official receptions mind-numbing and exhausting, having been taught as a child to address a few well-chosen remarks to every tree she passed on her daily walks.) As it turned out, the old Queen and the young governess found common cause in first Elizabeth, then Margaret.

As she had been with Allah, the Duchess was content to let Crawfie get on with the job as she saw fit. That troubled the governess, who 'worried a lot' at the responsibility forced on her.

In desperation she looked to Queen Mary for guidance. It was promptly given. The Queen became what Crawfie called a 'wonderful ally' as she battled to provide a practical educational foundation on which to build the Duchess's idealised notion of childhood, which was 'to spend as long as possible in the open air, to enjoy to the full the pleasure of the country, to be able to dance and appreciate music, to acquire good manners and perfect deportment, and to cultivate the feminine graces.'

There were many times, Crawfie said, when she turned to the Queen when she was in trouble. 'She was always a rock of

strength and wisdom to me; someone I could go to in moments of doubt and difficulty. There were to be plenty of both.' Less for Crawfie, as it happens, than for Queen Mary, who was having to face up to the consequences of the disturbingly irresponsible behaviour of her eldest son.

In the royal manner, nobody broke the code of discretion that cements his or her lips in silence by referring to the looming crisis. 'Maybe the general hope was that if nothing was said the whole business would blow over,' Crawfie said. It didn't. The Prince of Wales exchanged one married mistress for another, and then took up with the most undesirable one of all: Wallis Simpson. His wilful reluctance to find himself a suitable girlfriend who would make a suitable wife inevitably focused attention on the heiress presumptive, Princess Elizabeth.

It was vital, the old Queen ruled, that Elizabeth should study genealogy, that comedy of bloodlines running back to Queen Victoria that provided Europe with its royal houses.

History was important too, as were poetry ('wonderful memory training') and knowledge of the geography of the British Empire.

But mathematics? 'Was arithmetic really more valuable,' the Queen wanted to know, 'than history?' Money is not a subject of practical concern to the royal family; Elizabeth, the Queen observed with telling foresight, would probably never have to do her own household accounts.

BELOW: Princess Elizabeth, with her mother, grandmother and sister, attends the first Trooping the Colour of her father's reign, 14 June 1937

OPPOSITE PAGE: Following their coronation on 12 May 1937, George VI and Queen Elizabeth appear on the palace balcony with their daughters and Queen Mary

Crawfie took note. 'Queen Mary's practical suggestions were most welcome and I revised the schoolroom schedule for Princess Elizabeth accordingly.' Whether the Duchess ever knew about this, and if she did whether she cared, is not recorded. The answer in both cases is probably not. The Yorks, so determinedly bourgeois in all other things, simply did not consider education a matter of any great importance. 'No one ever had employers who interfered so little,' the governess noted.

What did concern the Yorks, just as much as it did Queen Mary, was the Prince of Wales's affair with Wallis Simpson. It was a liaison branded with the hallmark of catastrophe – for the country, for the Crown and for the Yorks themselves.

George V died on 20 January 1936 (by the hand of his doctor, it transpired, who administered him a lethal injection of cocaine to ensure that the announcement of his death would make the next morning's edition of *The Times* and not the less respectable evening papers). David was now King Edward VIII. The Crown's hold on him, however, was less than Mrs Simpson's, and he would soon let go of his birthright 'for the woman I love'.

Bertie, afflicted with a bad stammer and frail of health, did not want to shoulder the responsibility of kingship. He did not believe he was up to it. He had not been trained for it, he complained. A number of senior government advisors agreed, and when it became clear that a new king was going to have to be found, there was a suggestion, recorded in 1947 'by gracious permission of His Majesty the King' by Dermot Morrah, Fellow of All Souls College, Oxford, that the Crown should go to his younger brother, the Duke of Kent.

It was, however, only a suggestion. As far as most people were concerned, the Crown could only go to Bertie.

'This is absolutely desperate,' he cried to his cousin, the future Earl Mountbatten of Burma. 'I've never even seen a state paper.' (Another cousin, Nicholas II, expressed the same sentiments when the imperial crown of Russia came to him. 'What will happen to me?' the Tsar wailed. I'm not prepared to be a tsar. I never wanted to become one. I know nothing of the business of ruling. I have no idea of even how to talk to the ministers.')

The only real solution to the crisis threatening to engulf the Royal House of Windsor, however, was to pass the Crown to the next in line, however reluctant he might be to accept it. Some order had to be made of the chaos David's ill-considered affair had caused.

The future King later reported that when his mother broke the news to him that the uncrowned Edward VIII had done the unthinkable and abdicated the throne, passing his responsibilities to him: 'I broke down and sobbed like a child.' The Queen, needless to say, was highly embarrassed by such a display of weakness in yet another of her sons.

'Really!' she was heard to exclaim in the middle of the abdication crisis. 'This might be Romania.'

The Duchess had not been quite the support she might have been as events had moved towards their denouement. As the abdication approached she retired to bed ill – 'a not uncommon reaction, throughout her life, to moments of great stress', as royal biographer Robert Lacey later noted.

Faced with a situation from which there was no retreat, however, the new Queen Consort showed her mettle. She had not wanted to be Queen, but when the role was thrust upon her she assumed its mantle with grace and natural poise.

There was a dark personal side to this apparently blossoming public face. Bertie, now transmogrified into George VI, had always been prone to tantrums, known within his family as 'gnashes'. The confusion and fear engendered by this dramatic change in his position, and by the later worries caused by the war, served only to exacerbate his unsteady and sometimes violent temperament.

His father, George V, had been subject to similar temper fits. His married life was less than blissful, and the King and Queen found it so difficult to communicate that they had to write letters to each other instead.

Late in his life, Edward VIII, then Duke of Windsor, told author James Pope-Hennessy: 'Off the record, my father had a most horrible temper. He was foully rude to my mother. Why, I've seen her leave the table because he was so rude to her, and we children would all follow her out.'

The Duke added, 'Not when staff were present, of course.' But staff have a way of finding out about such things. George V's behaviour was well-discussed in the servants' quarters, as were George VI's outbursts.

Scenes of such private unhappiness and frustration were never played out in public. Nor, as far as it was possible to contain them, were they allowed to intrude on to the nursery floor. 'We want our children to have a happy childhood which they can always look back on,' Queen Elizabeth insisted.

The happy family idyll, however, had been damaged. The family were forced to move out of 145 Piccadilly and into Buckingham Palace, a cold, impersonal building with endless

corridors that could take a whole morning to navigate. Couldn't they build a tunnel back to Piccadilly, Elizabeth wistfully suggested? The real world, with its domestic upsets and feuds and subtleties of status and inexorable duty could not be locked out. The ritual of bathtime had to be changed because the Duke and Duchess, who before had spent most of their evenings at home, were now out almost every night at official functions.

The children, Elizabeth in particular, could not but be aware of the tensions – of the strain events had caused their father, of the way their mother, once so relaxed and easygoing, now looked drawn and older. There had also been a change in her own status. As a little girl, Elizabeth had been taught to curtsey to her grandparents whenever she visited them. The aura of majesty, in power even at home, had now fallen on her parents and she was instructed by Crawfie that henceforth they had to curtsey to Papa and Mummy.

'Margaret too?' Elizabeth asked. 'Margaret also,' was the answer. 'And try not to topple over.'

The King and his Queen Consort soon put a stop to that.

The ten-year-old Princess was not in any doubt about what her position was, though – and hadn't been for some years. Elizabeth, Crawfie insisted, was a 'special' child: neat, courteous, conscientious, unusually well-behaved and 'very shy'. She was aware from the earliest age of where she stood in the pecking order. Her parents wanted their daughter to feel a 'member of the community' but, as Crawfie remarked, 'just how difficult this is to achieve, if you live in a palace, is hard to explain. A glass curtain seems to come down between you and the outer world, between the hard realities of life and those who dwell in a court.'

When she played in Hamilton Gardens, crowds of people would gather to peer at her through the railings, as if they were contemplating an exotic creature at the zoo. When she went for walks in Hyde Park she was often recognised.

'Ignore them,' Allah ordered, following her own advice and striding purposefully past gawping onlookers, looking neither to left nor right. With Allah as her trainer, Elizabeth's ability to completely disregard the stares of the inquisitive soon became second nature. But she knew why they were looking.

LEFT: Elizabeth and Margaret with their cousin Jean Wills for the christening of her son, Arnold, at St Paul's Knightsbridge in October 1937

OPPOSITE PAGE: The Princesses accompany the King and Queen to a medals presentation in the garden at Buckingham Palace, 20 May 1937

When she was seven years old, Elizabeth was addressed by the Lord Chamberlain with a cheery, 'Good morning, little lady.'

'I'm not a little lady,' was the imperious reply. 'I'm Princess Elizabeth!'

This display of regal asperity proved too much for Queen Mary, who promptly marched her granddaughter into the Lord Chamberlain's office and said, 'This is Princess Elizabeth, who one day hopes to be a lady.'

But a princess she certainly was, and with her uncle gone and the likelihood of her parents producing a son and heir apparent receding with each passing year, a queen she was ever more likely to become. The impact of that impending burden only hardened her emotional restraint.

The death of George V had provoked no outward display of emotion, only the question whether it was right that she should continue playing with her toy horses. (Crawfie said it was.)

After she was taken to see her grandfather lying in state in Westminster Hall, she remarked: 'Uncle David was there and he never moved at all. Not even an eyelid. It was wonderful. And everyone was so quiet. As if the King were asleep.'

'She was reserved and quiet about her feelings,' Crawfie noted.

'I've been trained since childhood never to show emotion in public,' Elizabeth once remarked.

When Uncle David abdicated and the Crown was placed upon the reluctant head of their father, Margaret turned to her sister in the nursery at 145 Piccadilly and asked, 'Does that mean you will have to be the next queen?'

'Yes, some day,' Princess Elizabeth gravely replied.

Back came the response: 'Poor you.'

The girls spent the day looking down the stairwell at the comings and goings of the Prime Minister and his ministers, and then rushing to the windows to stare at the thousands of people gathered outside. When a letter was delivered addressed to Her Majesty The Queen, Princess

LEFT: Princess Elizabeth attends a daytime rehearsal of the Aldershot military tattoo in the summer of 1938

Elizabeth turned to Lady Cynthia Asquith. 'That's Mummy now,' she said, with a tremor in her voice.

Whatever awe she felt was offset by her inherent composure and her remarkable sense of responsibility. She was not worldly and has not become so. It was never intended that she should.

The practice of keeping her emotions to herself in public was carried over by force of habit into her private life. She does not like being touched. She raises her voice rarely; anger and temperament have no part to play in her lifetime's exercise in self-control. Instead she shows her displeasure by icy silence. If that makes her incomplete as a person – and there is an element of the child in her inability to address the sometimes wayward behaviour of her own family – there is also a regality about her that is both reassuring and intimidating. It is an aura of majesty that comes naturally to her. It was as if she always knew she was destined to be queen, and set about from the earliest age acquiring the necessary skills, always trying hard to do 'what she felt was expected of her'.

Elizabeth did not join Margaret in those practical jokes that are such a tradition in the royal family (as long ago as 1860, Lord Clarendon reported that he never told the royal family his best jokes because pretending to pinch his finger in the door amused them more). When Margaret hid the gardener's rake or threatened to sound the bell at Windsor that brought out the guard, Elizabeth would hide with embarrassment.

Order had to be maintained. She was, said Crawfie, 'neat and methodical beyond words'. She would sometimes get up in the middle of the night to make sure her shoes were neatly stowed.

Self-control was essential. At the Coronation of their father in Westminster Abbey, she said of her sister: 'I do hope she won't disgrace us all by falling asleep in the middle.' And when their parents set sail for the propaganda tour of Canada and the United States just before the outbreak of the Second World War, and Margaret told her that she had her handkerchief ready, Elizabeth sternly warned her 'to wave, not to cry'.

She was compassionate. During the war the two Princesses were moved to the comparative safety of Windsor Castle. They were subjected to the occasional air raid but never to the full force of the Blitz. Even so, Elizabeth took a keen and caring interest in the welfare of those more directly affected by the carnage. When the battleship HMS *Royal Oak* was sunk she exclaimed, 'It can't be! All those nice sailors.'

That Christmas she remarked, 'Perhaps we are too happy. I keep thinking of those sailors and what Christmas must have been like in their homes.' And when she read the name of someone she knew, usually an officer who had been stationed briefly at Windsor Castle, she would write to the man's mother, Crawfie revealed, 'and give her a little picture of how much she had appreciated him and what they had talked about'. The governess confirmed: 'That was entirely her own idea.'

More mundanely but very much in character, she would instruct her more rumbustious sister not to point and laugh at anyone wearing a 'funny hat'.

Elizabeth subscribed to Louis XIV's view that punctuality is the politeness of princes (and princesses) and was always on time. She was obedient – her only transgression of any note, apart from the occasional nursery scrap with her sister, was when she was seven or eight years old: she tipped an ornamental ink pot over her own head during a French lesson.

She was discreet. When the King flew to Italy in 1944 he told his daughter where he was going. His trip was classified as top secret and Elizabeth kept the information to herself and didn't even share it with the women – Allah, Bobo and Crawfie – she was so close to. She also acquired the royal family habit of banishing unpleasant thoughts and people from her mind. They simply ceased to exist.

'Uncle David was not dead,' Crawfie wrote. He might as well have been. The Duke of Windsor had been particularly fond of his niece. He had been a frequent visitor to the house in Piccadilly and took a childish delight in joining her in her games. Since the abdication he had ceased to exist for her.

'In the Palace and the Castle his name was never mentioned,' Crawfie noted.

Now that the Crown was all but certain to pass to her, her father, from the day he became George VI, started taking his daughter into his confidence, 'speaking to her as an equal'. By war's end she was attending council meetings, taking the counsel of Prime Minister Winston Churchill and discussing affairs of state with her father on a daily basis.

Queen Elizabeth also renewed her interest in her daughter's education, and it was at her instigation that she was sent to study constitutional history under Sir Henry Marten, the Vice-Provost of Eton College, across the Thames from Windsor.

Yet for all Elizabeth's maturity she remained in many ways a child. Her polished manners and grown-up conversation concealed a wealth of inexperience. Throughout her childhood and almost all of her teens, she was dressed in similar clothes to her sister, who was all of four years her junior. She also shared her nursery classroom with Margaret. She never had to hone her talents competing with her contemporaries.

Isolated behind that glass curtain, she enjoyed little social life of her own. What she did have she left to her mother to organise. It was not until a special Girl Guides troop was formed for her that her circle widened to include children from beyond her own privileged background.

A number of cockney evacuees from the East End of London joined the royal troop at Windsor. It was 'no doubt very instructive,' Crawfie remarked, for Elizabeth to mix with youngsters who did not have a 'tendency to let them have an advantage, win a game, or be relieved of the more sordid tasks', as the children of the court had.

Now, said Crawfie, 'it was each for himself'. The Princess was far from comfortable in this competitive environment. She liked the security of the safe and simple routine of royal life. Ever since she was a little girl she had shared her bedroom with Bobo Macdonald, the Scotswoman 22 years her senior who became and remained her closest friend. Elizabeth found the informal intimacy of a Guides camp difficult to deal with.

'She was getting older, and had been brought up so much alone,' Crawfie said.

'I could understand why she did not want to undress before a lot of children all of a sudden, and spend the night with them.'

When it came to dealing with boys she was even more inhibited. Boys of any kind, Crawfie noted, were strange creatures out of another world to the Princess and her sister. Margaret was instinctively flirtatious in the company of the opposite sex, whereas fundamentally shy Elizabeth was always much more reserved.

'That unsophisticated air of hers has always been part of her charm,' her governess remarked.

When she was under the tutelage of Sir Henry Marten in his study at Eton, his regular pupils would sometimes look in but they, with typical Etonian insouciance, feigned not to know who she was, and after

politely raising their top hats would speedily withdraw again. Elizabeth, for her part, pretended not to notice the interruptions.

At the age of almost 18 she 'had not yet attained the full allure of an adult', according to her father's equerry, Group Captain Peter Townsend. 'She was shy, occasionally to the point of gaucheness.'

No real attempt was made to put her more at ease with young men. Miss Betty Vacani, the London dancing mistress who would also teach the next royal generation their steps, was invited to Windsor during the war to organise dance classes for Elizabeth and Margaret. By royal command they were for little girls only.

'The Princesses did not understand the antics of little boys, and this did not seem the moment to teach them,' Crawfie said.

There was one boy Elizabeth did notice, however. He was tall and blond, with 'Viking' good looks. His name was Prince Philip of Greece and she was dazzled by him from the first moment she saw him.

She was 13 at the time, he 18. They married eight years later. He was the only man she had ever known.

Elizabeth spent the night before she was married in her nursery bedroom. On the morning of her wedding she came out of the nursery, paused to say goodbye to the toy horses that had followed her from the house in Piccadilly and were stabled in the corridor outside, and then spent a few minutes with her parents, as she had done every morning since she was a baby.

In a very literal sense Elizabeth Alexandra Mary, named after three queens and soon to be one herself, went straight from the nursery to the marital bed.

RIGHT: On her 13th birthday, Elizabeth goes riding in the Great Park with the King and Margaret

OPPOSITE PAGE: The Princesses appear in uniform for the first time when they accompany their mother to a parade of 1,000 Girl Guides at Windsor Castle in June 1938

A sign of things to come:
Prince Philip of Greece and
Denmark in a sailor suit

Philip

PRINCE PHILIP'S CHILDHOOD was confused and rootless. It couldn't have got off to a more inauspicious start: he was born on 10 June 1921, on the island of Corfu, on the dining-room table of a house called, most ironically, Mon Repos. His father, Prince Andrew of Greece, had no money and the house lacked electricity, gas and running hot water, but Philip could at least consider himself lucky to have a father.

Greece was at war with Turkey. Greek advance had turned into crushing Turkish victory, and by the autumn of 1922 the Greeks had been driven out of Asia Minor, so ending a presence there that dated back 2,500 years.

Smyrna, the main Greek town on the Asian mainland, had been sacked, the young Aristotle Onassis had escaped and fled to Argentina to start his own meteoric social climb, and Prince Andrew had been arrested, charged with treason and was facing death by firing squad.

'How many children do you have,' Greece's military leader, General Pangalos, asked his royal prisoner.

'Five,' the Prince replied.

'Poor little orphans,' said the general.

The only advantage Andrew had was that he was a relation of the British royal family, but that might have proved no advantage at all had not King George V been consumed by the memory of what had happened to his Romanov relations four years earlier.

Marion Crawford, governess of Philip's future wife, made a point of teaching history as 'the doings not of a lot of dusty lay figures in the past, but of real people with all their problems and bothers'. The dust of silence had deliberately been allowed to settle over certain incidents in the royal family's recent history, however; Crawfie certainly did not apprise the young Elizabeth of them – and certainly not of the fatal part her grandfather had played in their tragic outcome.

In 1917 Russia had fallen to the Bolsheviks and Tsar Nicholas II had been deposed. He was George V's first cousin (their mothers were sisters); the men knew each other well and were on friendly terms, sometimes meeting, frequently exchanging letters. They even looked alike.

'Exactly like a skinny Duke of York [the future George V] – the image of him,' one of Queen Victoria's ladies-in-waiting once observed of Nicholas. When Nicholas appealed to his cousin for asylum in Britain, however, George V made it his personal business to ensure that it was refused.

Where would he stay, the King wanted to know? And who was going to pay for his upkeep?

The Prime Minister, David Lloyd George, had offered the imperial family the sanctuary they sought. The King, however, aware of the social instability and the corresponding upsurge in republicanism the First World War had generated in Britain, was concerned that Nicholas would bring Russia's revolutionary chaos with him.

Sacrificing family blood on the altar of expediency, he ordered his private secretary, Lord Stamfordham, to write to the Foreign Secretary, Lord Balfour: 'The residence in this country of the ex-Emperor and his Empress... would undoubtedly compromise the position of the King and Queen.'

The offer was duly withdrawn, and on 16 July 1918 Nicholas, his wife Alexandra, their four daughters and young son were shot and bayoneted to death in a cellar in Ekaterinburg in the Urals. There is no record of George V expressing sorrow, much less contrition, at his own role in the tragedy.

But now another royal relation – and one who also had a wife, four daughters and a young son – was facing execution. It was a matter the King could not ignore.

Andrew, like the murdered Tsar, was also a first cousin; his father, George I of Greece, was the brother of George and Nicholas's mothers. There were other connections: Andrew's wife was Alice of Battenberg, daughter of the former First Sea Lord, who changed his name to Mountbatten and became 1st Marquess of Milford Haven.

Once described as 'the prettiest Princess in Europe', Alice was a great-granddaughter of Queen Victoria, the niece of Nicholas's murdered wife, Alix, and a first cousin once removed of George V himself.

Andrew – self-opinionated and with an eye for the ladies – had to accept a large part of the responsibility for the final disaster that seemed set to befall him and his family.

He wasn't Greek at all. The family were Danish, if anything, though it would be more accurate to describe him as a member of an inter-related tribe of German princelings who had come to occupy all the thrones of Europe.

But he was the grandson of the King of Greece and, more pertinently, an officer in the Greek army.

At the outbreak of hostilities with Turkey in 1921, he was a major-general with command of a division stationed in Asia Minor. His troops were 'riff-raff', he declared, his officers useless, the high command incapable.

His assessment was accurate though hardly diplomatic. Nor was it the height of military professionalism to disobey the clear and direct order to advance and instead ask to be relieved of one's command.

When Smyrna fell and his family were again ousted – a regular occurrence since they had first been invited on to the throne of Greece in

RIGHT: Philip in 1922, shortly after his first birthday. Later that year he and his family had to leave their Corfu home

1863 – Andrew provided the new military rulers with a made-to-measure scapegoat. He was arrested, tried and sentenced by a jury of junior officers who had, Princess Alice decided, 'previously decided that he must be shot'.

George V had been prepared to leave the Romanovs to their fate, but the idea of allowing another batch of close relations to fall to the executioner's blade or bullet clearly proved too much to stomach even for a monarch as imperious as he. Following appeals by Princess Alice through her younger brother, Louis, the future Earl Mountbatten of Burma, the King personally ordered that his incautious relation was for saving.

Commander Gerald Talbot, Britain's former naval attaché in Athens, now employed as a secret agent in Geneva, was duly dispatched, in disguise and travelling under false papers, to open negotiations with Pangalos. They did not go well until the cruiser HMS *Calypso* sailed in, guns raised, to help concentrate the military government's thoughts.

Which it did: while Andrew's fellow prisoners were being duly executed, he was driven to the harbour by Pangalos himself and put aboard *Calypso*, where his wife was waiting for him.

The warship then steamed to Corfu to pick up 18-month-old Prince Philip and his four sisters. The family were quite philosophical about being exiled, 'for they frequently are', as *Calypso*'s captain, Buchanan-Wollaston, observed.

Philip's sister, Princess Sophie, about eight at the time, was not so sanguine. 'It was a terrible business, absolute chaos,' she later recalled.

The crossing to Brindisi in Italy was a rough one and the family, their Greek lady-in-waiting, French governess and English nanny, Emily Roose, were all seasick.

Once ashore they took the train from Brindisi to Rome and then to Paris. Philip spent much of the journey crawling around on the floor, blackening himself from head to toe and even licking the windowpanes. His mother tried to restrain him but Nana Roose – 'A divine person, much nicer than all the other nannies, we adored her,' Sophie remembered – kindly advised, 'Leave him alone.'

'He was *very* active,' said the Princess.

Philip's life until then had been one of distinctly unroyal disorder. Mon Repos, built in 1832 by a British governor, Sir Frederick Ashton, for his Greek wife, was in 'wretched' decay; the staff (with the exception of the English nanny, whom Philip called 'Roosie') slovenly.

They did not live like royals,' their housekeeper recalled. 'We had a few untrained peasant girls to help, and two unwashed footmen who were rough fellows.'

Nor could it be said that the squalor was offset by a happy atmosphere. Philip's father had been arrested and dragged away in front of his weeping family to face trial and the threat of execution; his mother, meanwhile, was heading towards a nervous breakdown. But Mon Repos, for all its drawbacks, was at least a family home, and that was something that Philip would not experience again until he married the future Queen.

Exiled, poor (they had to borrow money for the train fare to Paris from the British ambassador to Italy, Sir Ronald Graham), forced to rely on the charity of relations, a few friends and those still impressed enough by their royal status to pay for their company (the family didn't even have a proper surname), they were condemned to join the litter of dispossessed princelings strewn across Europe between the wars.

At the age of three months Philip had been taken to London for the funeral of his grandfather, the 1st Marquess of Milford Haven, where he had met his uncles, David and Louis, for the first time. Despite the proliferation of relations there, England was not deemed a suitable place for their exile. Questions had been asked in the House of Commons about the use of a British warship in their rescue – an argument over who should shoulder the costs dragged on between the Treasury and the Admiralty for several years – and it was deemed 'undesirable' by the King and the government that they should come to England 'at the present time'. Instead they set up camp in Paris, first in an apartment, then at St Cloud, the lodge in the grounds of the house owned by his uncle Prince George's wife, Princess Marie Bonaparte, great-granddaughter of Napoleon's brother, Lucien.

It was a foundering, fragmented existence. Philip's parents drifted apart. His father spent his time in cafés, plotting never-to-be-enacted coups to restore his family to the Greek throne, before eventually drifting off to Monte Carlo and out of his son's life to set up home with a widowed actress. When Philip was ten, his mother had her long-threatened nervous breakdown.

Deaf from birth, Princess Alice had overcome her physical handicap, had learned to lip-read in four languages, and had been a vivacious and enchanting young woman. The struggles of exile proved beyond her, however, and after several unsuccessful treatments in Swiss sanatoria she re-emerged in a nun's habit that she wore for the rest of her life. She founded her own order, the Christian Sisterhood of Martha and Mary, and all but withdrew from the world.

Prince Philip saw little of her or his father; it was his sisters and the indefatigable Nanny Roose who bore the responsibility for his upbringing. Nanny had the greatest influence. 'Nobody's allowed to spank me but my own nanny,' he informed a friend's nanny who was about to discipline him for breaking an expensive vase.

Among his closest friends was Hélène Foufounis, whose royalist grandfather was also in exile and was rich enough to help the financially-troubled Prince Andrew. Like Philip, she too eventually moved to Britain where, as Hélène Cordet, she became a London cabaret singer and nightclub owner, and remained one of his close confidantes.

'He was like an English boy rather than a Greek or German,' she recalled. 'He had an English nanny.'

When Philip was born Nanny Roose had ordered supplies of British soap, British baby food and British woollies to be despatched to Mon Repos. She taught him British nursery rhymes and despite the lack of funds insisted on dressing him in clothes sent from London.

And she made absolutely certain that he 'spoke English and was brought up with English customs'. Superficially, that is. For there was nothing English about the lack of order or stability in Philip's childhood.

Holidays were spent rattling across Europe by train to stay with those relations who had managed to hang on to their possessions.

To Romania, for instance, where his aunt Missy was Queen (she wore a tiara at dinner every evening) and where Philip's cousin Queen Alexandra of Yugoslavia remembered 'our nannies all cheerfully sitting down to tea with bowls of caviar'.

The young boy whose own means were so straitened was allowed no such extravagance.

He was trained, Alexandra revealed, 'to save and economise better than other children – so much so that he acquired a reputation for being mean'.

Philip had other advantages, though. He was handsome. 'Everyone adored him so much, particularly my mother, because he was so good looking,' Hélène Cordet recalled.

'He had such unbelievable charm,' said his sister, Sophie. 'He had a tremendous sense of humour.'

He was a 'real' boy with an adventurous, outgoing personality, fond of climbing trees, forever testing himself against the elements and his playmates.

'It was always Philip,' Alexandra said, 'who ventured out of his depth' at the seaside, 'or who rounded up other boys encountered on the beach and organised an intensive castle-building brigade'.

He was given a Box Brownie and took up photography, which remained a lifetime's hobby. He had a boy's interest in motorcars.

Philip's humour was of a rumbustious kind. 'He was a great show-off; he would stand on his head when visitors came', one of his sisters remarked.

On one occasion while staying with another aunt, Queen Sophie of Greece, and her sister, the Landgravine of Hesse, Alexandra saw him release a sty of pigs and stampede them through the ladies' elegant garden party.

Philip apparently has no recollection of that incident.

But he could be kind-hearted. When a rich cousin, who was very taken with Philip, once bought him a toy, she cruelly said to Hélène's nine-year-old sister, Ria, who was stricken with a diseased hip: 'I didn't buy you anything because you can't play.'

'Philip went red and ran out of the room,' Hélène said, 'He came back with an armful of his own toys, and the new one, thrust them on the bed and said, "These are for you".'

LEFT: A studio portrait of Prince Philip, with his trademark blond locks, at the age of three

OPPOSITE PAGE: Princess Andrew of Greece and her son in 1924, by which time they were living in France

Later, at Salem School, he encountered the viciousness inherent in the new Nazi Germany. One boy, Philip remembered, 'so displeased the thugs that they caught him… and shaved his head. I lent him my Cheam 2nd XI cap and I hope he has got it still.'

Such engaging high points, revealing as they are in isolation, should not be allowed to obscure the uncertainty that characterised his childhood as a whole. Or the fact that, for all his hearty high spirits, he was sometimes rude and always academically lazy.

The Prince's early education was not notable for its classroom successes. At the age of six he was sent to the MacJannet American School in Paris. Philip rode there on a bicycle he had bought himself with savings that had started with the £1 his uncle, the King of Sweden, sent him every year. His school report called him 'rugged, boisterous'.

At the age of eight, in educational confirmation of his 'Englishness', he was sent to Cheam Preparatory School outside London. There he won the school diving competition, came equal first in the high jump, won the under-12 hurdles and became an 'improved' cricketer. But again he failed to shine academically.

He did win the Form III French prize, but, as his cousin Alexandra told him, so he should have, 'after all the years he had lived in Paris'. He had been sent to Cheam on the advice of his uncle, George, 2nd Marquess of Milford Haven, who had been sent there in turn by his father, who had been impressed by the good manners of two Cheam-educated midshipmen.

RIGHT: The future Duke of Edinburgh, spade in hand, on a beach with his parents

OPPOSITE PAGE: Philip (second left) with schoolmates at the MacJannet American School in St Cloud

Milford Haven's own son, David, who was two years older than Philip, also went there and the two became firm friends.

The fees to send him to these two expensive schools had been provided first by Prince George of Greece and the Marquess of Milford Haven. Both men were married to women who formed an important part of his female support system, though given their sexual proclivities one can only imagine what kind of influence these benefactresses had on the young boy.

Marie Bonaparte, besides being the great-great-niece of Napoleon, was also the granddaughter of François Blanc, the founder of the Monte Carlo casino, who ended up as virtual owner of the principality and used his newly-acquired wealth to buy his daughter a titled husband. His granddaughter had inherited not only a sizeable part of his Monte Carlo-made fortune but also a morality that went well with that Ruritania on the Riviera, which Somerset Maugham called 'a sunny place for shady people'. She was notoriously promiscuous, had been subjected to blackmail and included Aristide Briand, several times Prime Minister of France, amongst her lovers.

Nada, the Marchioness of Milford Haven, was equally unconventional. The daughter of Grand Duke Michael of Russia, the former Countess Nadejda de Torby was a great-granddaughter of the poet Pushkin. Dark and beautiful, she was accused, in one of the most lurid trials of the 1930s, of being the lesbian lover of the heiress Gloria Vanderbilt.

When Gloria went to court to fight for the custody of her daughter – the original 'poor little rich girl' and also called Gloria – Mrs Vanderbilt's former maid took the stand to testify that she had seen the Marchioness embrace her employer 'like a lover'. Her husband, for his part, was an avid collector of early sexual aids and pornography.

Philip spent his holidays from Cheam at the Milford Havens' home, Lynden Manor, near Windsor.

Great emphasis has been placed on Uncle 'Dickie' Mountbatten's role in Philip's upbringing. 'I don't think anybody thinks I had a father. Most people think that Dickie is my father anyway,' he said. In reality Mountbatten played no part until much later, and then rather less than he liked to make out. 'Mountbatten certainly had an influence on the

course of my life, but not so much on my ideas and attitudes,' Philip informed the author Tim Heald. 'I suspect he tried too hard to make himself a son out of me.' It was in fact Louis's brother, George Milford Haven, who 'assumed the role of a surrogate father' to the boy.

Indeed, at the time, the exotic Milford Havens were his only family, for between December 1930, when he was nine years old, and August 1931, shortly after he had turned ten, his four sisters, all members of the German aristocracy, left to start households of their own. The family dispersal, which had started when they left Greece on the *Calypso*, had turned into a diaspora that left Philip without a home, a mother or the protective affection of his sisters.

If this wasn't problematic enough, tragedy started to crowd in. In 1937 his third sister, Cecile, and her husband, George Donatus of Hesse, flew to London for the wedding of George's brother, Louis, to Lord Geddes' daughter, Margaret.

Over Ostend the plane hit a factory chimney. Cecile, her husband – to whom Philip had been particularly attached – their two children and the unborn child Cecile was carrying

were among those killed. Their surviving daughter, who had been too young to make the flight, died of meningitis two years later.

In 1938, when Philip was 17, George Milford Haven died of cancer at the age of 46.

By now Philip no longer even had his nanny to turn to. His beloved Roosie, now well into her seventies, had contracted arthritis and retired to the sunshine of South Africa.

Philip could have been forgiven for thinking that the fates were closing in on him, but he dismissed that notion. He was big and athletic and capable of looking after himself; his independence had been forged on the anvil of a harsh environment.

His childhood, he insisted, was 'not particularly unhappy'. The disruption of exile, he maintained, did not concern him. 'I was barely a year old when the family went into exile so I don't think I suffered the same disorientation,' he said.

And if his home life had been unsettled, so what. 'People talk about a normal upbringing. What is a normal upbringing?' he once demanded gruffly.

The first thing Kurt Hahn, his headmaster at Gordonstoun, noted was his 'undefeatable spirit'.

Child psychologists might see such determined self-reliance in a different light. Mussen, Conger and Kagan, in *Child Development and Personality*, theorise on the emotional state of an overtly independent child thus: 'Because he has never experienced a continuous loving relationship or, more frequently, because the relationship he has had has been disrupted so severely, he has not only reached but remained in a phase of detachment.

'As a result he remains dead and incapable of experiencing separation, anxiety or grief. Lesser degrees of this condition are, of course, more common than the extreme degrees, and sometimes give the impression of unusually vigorous independence. Analysis shows that the springs of love are frozen and their independence is hollow.'

RIGHT: A signed photograph of eight-year-old Philip in Greek national costume, which he presented to his headmaster

OPPOSITE PAGE: The Prince, *centre of group*, in the grounds of his school in the Paris suburb of St Cloud

Such academic theorising would probably have been dismissed by the young Philip, who was fond of saying that he was 'one of those ignorant bums who never went to university – and a fat lot of harm it did me!' He was not much given to self-analysis. He was what he was. But who exactly was he?

'He was very aware of his position and we were too,' said Hélène Cordet.

'You could not forget who he was. He had been brought up to realise he was a prince.'

There were moments, though, when the Prince seemed determined to rid himself of his royal appellation.

Hélène's mother, Anna, recalled how he hated being introduced as Prince Philip, grandson of the King of Greece.

'I'm just Philip. Just Philip, that's all!' he would shout.

Louis Mountbatten expended a great deal of energy inventing a magnificent pedigree for himself that traced his ancestry back to Charlemagne yet disingenuously overlooked the fact that his grandmother was not royal at all. Or that he was therefore the progeny of a morganatic union which had stripped his family of their royal A-rating.

The personal success Mountbatten achieved – and he enjoyed a glorious career: Supreme Allied Commander, South East Asia, during the Second World War; Viceroy of India; First Sea Lord; an earldom – did not exorcise his ancestral demons. Quite the contrary; it seemed to fuel his naked snobbery.

'We always took Dickie with a pinch of salt,' Queen Elizabeth the Queen Mother once remarked witheringly.

Philip took a more balanced view of his bloodline. Being royal, as he knew from his own experience, provided no guarantee of future employment.

It could be a handicap as well as an advantage. It had given him a title and opened the palace doors of Europe to him, but it had also deprived him of a home and a stable family life.

Yet, despite his insistence that he be called Philip and not Prince Philip, royal he was. It was written into his family's genealogical past and future ambition. Even as an impecunious youngster in France he seemed to have an instinctive appreciation of where his destiny lay.

'Some day I'll be an important man – a king even!' he told Hélène Cordet's brother, Jean.

Philip had no interest in returning to Greece. 'A grandfather assassinated and a father condemned to death does not endear me to the perpetrators.'

Instead he looked to Britain, his mother's homeland, to which he had become very attached. At the end of one visit to her relations in England, Princess Alice had had to drag him out from under a bed and sedate him to get him on the train back to France.

After Cheam he had been sent to Salem, the school founded in 1920 by his sister Theodora's father-in-law, Prince Max of Baden, and formulated by his former secretary, Kurt Hahn.

It was their attempt to rebuild a war-torn Germany's manhood by educating them along British public school lines with a dollop of Plato thrown in. The early Thirties were not the ideal time for a school whose ambition, as Prince Max put it, was to 'train soldiers who are at the same time lovers of peace'.

LEFT: Philip rides with his cousin King Michael of Romania on the sands at Constanza, 1928

OPPOSITE PAGE: The far-from-studious Prince at his desk in the schoolroom

Prince Max, the last chancellor of imperial Germany, had arranged the Kaiser's abdication. But now a new chancellor was in power in the Reichstag and his name was Adolf Hitler. Philip, too 'international' as he described himself, did not settle in well under this regime of muscular chauvinism.

He found the Nazi salute hilarious. It reminded him, he said, of the gesture his Cheam classmates would make when they wanted to be excused to go to the lavatory. He found the organised bullying of the party faithful offensive.

Some of his in-laws became high officials in the Nazi regime. The Badens did not. 'As none of that family was at all enthusiastic about them [the Nazis] it was thought best I should move out,' Philip explained in 1990.

In 1933 Hahn, a Jew as well as a radical thinker, was arrested. On his release he fled to Britain where he opened another school the following year. It was called Gordonstoun, and Philip was one of his first 30 pupils.

Hahn – the Prince called him 'eccentric perhaps, innovator certainly, great beyond doubt'– believed in body over mind, physical endeavour over the academic.

It is not an educational system that suits everyone. The sensitive – Prince Charles, for instance – can find it hard to come to terms with Teutonic austerity.

But it suited Philip and he thrived in the tough, Spartan environment Hahn created for his acolytes on the windswept coast of Scotland's Moray Firth. It developed and confirmed his sense of independence. He became, as one of his authorised biographers observed, 'his own man, anxious to learn and be advised but, in the end, taking his own decisions in his own way'.

It is a trait that can make Philip appear rude and arrogant, as someone who has little sympathy for those less self-sufficient than he is. It is also a characteristic that seems to need the fuel of competition.

RIGHT: Smartly-dressed Philip with members of his family at the wedding of his sister Cecile in Darmstadt, 1931

OPPOSITE PAGE: Later that year the Prince attended the wedding of sister Theodora to Berthold, Margrave of Baden

In his final judgement of his star pupil, Hahn reported: 'His best is outstanding; but his second best is not good enough. Prince Philip will make his mark in any profession but will have to prove himself in a full trial of strength.'

The full trial of strength was contained at Gordonstoun, where the system is designed to make pupils compete, not with each other but with themselves. He was taught to sail, for instance, and he thrived on the challenge.

'I was wet, cold, miserable, probably sick and often scared stiff,' he would later recall, 'but I wouldn't have missed the experience for anything. In any case the discomfort was far outweighed by moments of intense happiness and excitement.

'Poets and authors down the centuries have tried to describe those moments but their descriptions, however brilliant, will never compare with one's own experience.'

It was the air rather than the sea which most appealed to him as a career, however.

'I'd have gone into the Air Force without a doubt,' he said.

It was at this juncture that Lord Mountbatten assumed a guiding role in his nephew's life. He persuaded him not to join the RAF, but to follow family tradition and enter the Royal Navy. And that set in motion the chain of events that would secure his future.

In July 1939, the Royal Yacht *Victoria and Albert* sailed up the Dart to visit the Royal Naval College at Dartmouth. Aboard were George VI, his Queen, Elizabeth, and their two daughters, Elizabeth and Margaret. Mountbatten was in attendance. Waiting to greet them was the young cadet, Philip of Greece.

The college was afflicted with an outbreak of mumps and the King ruled that the two Princesses should not be allowed to mix with cadets. On Mountbatten's instigation, Philip was delegated to look after them. They played together with a clockwork train-set laid out in the captain's house; then, when 18-year-old Philip tired of that, went to the tennis courts where he impressed 13-year-old Elizabeth by jumping over the nets.

'How good he is, Crawfie. How high he can jump,' Princess Elizabeth whispered to her governess.

When the *Victoria and Albert* set sail that evening a number of naval cadets rowed after it. Philip – a 'rather bumptious boy' in Crawfie's opinion – rowed further and longer than anyone else. Eventually the King shouted: 'The young fool. He must go back, otherwise we will have to heave to and send him back.'

Philip was good-looking, 'rather like a Viking', Crawfie gushed, 'though rather offhand in his manner'. He would employ those looks to some effect over the next few years. He had, said his cousin Alexandra, a sailor's eye for a pretty face: 'Blondes, brunettes and redhead charmers, Philip gallantly – and I think quite impartially – squired them all.'

The dynastic die was cast that summer afternoon in Devon. Mountbatten undoubtedly played his part, but it would have been to no avail had Philip – talented, determined but poor – not done his bit.

Early in 1940 Prince Philip was posted to the battleship *Ramillies*, which was working as an escort vessel in the Mediterranean under the command of Vice-Admiral Harold Baillie-Grohman. According to one account, Baillie-Grohman pointed out to the Prince that unless he became a British subject he would not be allowed to advance very far in rank in the Royal Navy. Did he want to get on in the Navy, Baillie-Grohman asked.

'Yes' was the emphatic rejoinder. Philip then added: 'My uncle Dickie has ideas for me; he thinks I could marry Princess Elizabeth... I write to her every week.'

In 1941 Alexandra remembers him writing a letter. 'Who's it to?' she asked.

'Lilibet, Princess Elizabeth in England.'

'But she's only a baby,' his cousin exclaimed.

'Perhaps I'm going to marry her,' Philip replied.

The Prince later insisted that the question of marriage did not enter his mind before 1946 when he went to stay at Balmoral. 'I suppose one thing led to another. It was sort of fixed up.'

Sir Henry 'Chips' Channon, the American who married into the Guinness family, became an MP and kept a copious diary, believed it was 'fixed up' long before that.

Channon was in Athens in January 1941 when Philip, then 19, happened to be there on shore leave. Channon was a society butterfly who made it his business to know everyone. After a chat with Philip's aunt, Princess Nicholas of Greece, he recorded in his diary: He is to be our Prince Consort, and that is why he is serving in our Navy.'

George VI, his court and his government had their doubts. 'He's not English,' Princess Margaret observed.

Nevertheless, on 20 November 1947, and despite the initial and in part extreme reservations of those involved, the handsome, worldly sailor married the shy, ingenuous Princess. Philip dropped his Greek title, to which he had never been attached, and became Duke of Edinburgh and, eventually, a British prince.

After 26 years of rootless wandering, the exile who entered the world on a dining-room table was a fully-fledged member of the grandest royal family of all.

RIGHT: Philip at Gordonstoun, c.1937. The sports-loving Prince was captain of the hockey team

OPPOSITE PAGE: Philip, tossing the ball in the air, was also captain of the cricket team at the Morayshire public school

Charles

PRINCE CHARLES CELEBRATED his fourth birthday with a party in the white-and-gold Music Room at Buckingham Palace. Fourteen children were invited and the adjacent Picture Gallery was cleared of its impedimenta of chairs and tables and busts so that the Prince and his guests could run up and down.

On the West Terrace below, the band of the Grenadier Guards entertained the youthful revellers with a selection of nursery rhymes and then, as a special treat, with a rendition of Charles's favourite song, *The Teddy Bears' Picnic*.

There were two cakes. One was shaped as a galleon in full sail with marzipan masts and sweets in the hold; the other, a gift from the Queen Mother, was made in the form of Hansel and Gretel's cottage. His presents included a pedal car.

It was, so one observer recounted, 'the lightest-hearted party given at Buckingham Palace since the period of the Crimean War when Queen Victoria still had children young enough to romp in the same spirit'.

It was also notable for a shift in the royal approach to parenting: this was the first time Prince Philip had been present at one of his son's birthdays.

Charles had seen little of his father in his first formative years. He would soon see less of his mother, though for very different reasons.

Elizabeth had looked forward to motherhood. 'After all, it's what we're made for,' she said.

As a child she had declared that she wanted to marry a farmer, live in the country, have lots of animals and four children, two boys and two girls. She had married a sailor instead, but she had the animals and the country estates and their farming interests and she would eventually fulfil the last ambition, albeit with three boys and one girl.

Her greatest wish, she said, was for her children to be brought up to be 'normal'. She would often confide to Eileen Parker, whose husband, Michael, was equerry to the Princess and her husband and later Philip's private secretary, 'I would like them to live "ordinary" lives. I wish I could be more like you, Eileen.'

Elizabeth may have harboured doubts about her own upbringing – about its formality and protocol – but her confidante was not entirely convinced: 'I pondered, how much of a price would a princess truly be willing to pay in order to bring her children up like "ordinary people"?'

When it came to the routine of child rearing, not very much, it seemed.

Elizabeth suffered the discomforts of morning sickness during the early part of pregnancy. Charles was born at Buckingham Palace on the evening of 14 November 1948. Philip, a typically nervous expectant father, played a game of squash with Mike Parker to occupy himself during the waiting time and then went for a swim in the palace pool. He was just drying himself when a footman hurried in with the news that the Princess had given birth.

Hair still wet, Philip rushed up to the drawing room where the King and Queen were already receiving congratulations. Leaving his equerry to hand round the champagne, he went in to see his wife and newborn son. She was still under anaesthetic. When she came round Philip presented her with the bouquet of red roses and carnations that Parker had had the foresight to have ready.

Like all mothers, Elizabeth examined the baby's features, looking for family resemblances. She was struck by his hands. 'They are rather large, but fine with long fingers – quite unlike mine and certainly unlike his father's,' she wrote. 'It will be interesting to see what they will become. I still find it difficult to believe that I have a baby of my own.'

OPPOSITE PAGE: Prince Charles poses for an eighth-birthday portrait in the doorway of one of the state rooms at Buckingham Palace

Philip's opinion was typically blunt. Asked what his newborn son reminded him of he replied, 'A plum pudding.'

The boy was christened Charles Philip Arthur George in the Music Room where four years later he would host his first proper party. His godparents were George VI; his great-grandmother, Queen Mary; his aunt, Princess Margaret; his paternal great-grandmother, Victoria, Marchioness of Milford Haven; his great-uncle, David Bowes Lyon; Patricia Brabourne, Earl Mountbatten's daughter; Prince George of Greece; and King Haakon of Norway.

Elizabeth breastfed her young son for the first few weeks and Charles spent the first month of his life in a round wicker basket in the dressing room adjoining his mother's bedroom. Then, according to the dictates of circumstance and tradition, he was taken away from his mother and handed into the care of Nanny Helen Lightbody and the nursery maid, Mabel Anderson. Two world wars had delivered a hammer blow to the cosy, upper-class world of servants and nurseries. The royal family, however, secure in their time warp, had weathered the changes and Charles soon fell into the routine that had been so much part of Elizabeth's own childhood.

He was taken to see his mother every morning at nine – just as she had been taken to see her parents. And in the evenings, engagements permitting, she would join him for bath time, which he came to love (he thoroughly enjoyed playing with his plastic yellow ducks and a toy submarine). But that was just about the extent of it. After the first flush of involvement, the mundane chores of motherhood, like nappy-changing, were usually left to the nursery staff.

To my knowledge she never bathed the children,' Mrs Parker said. 'Nanny did all that.'

LEFT: Four generations – Queen Mary, George VI, Elizabeth and Charles – for his christening on 15 December 1948

OPPOSITE PAGE: The future Queen with her infant son at Buckingham Palace shortly before Christmas 1948

'A woman's paramount duty is to the home,' the Queen once opined. 'It is there she finds her truest fulfilment.' But as his heir, Elizabeth was forced to assume more and more of her ailing father's public duties, and that inevitably left less time for her son and his sister, Anne, who was born 21 months later.

The situation could only get worse once she had ascended the throne and her children's upbringing, as her own had been, was left in the care of the nursery staff. It was therefore to his nannies that Charles, who soon revealed himself to be a shy and sensitive child, turned for the affection he needed.

Both Nanny Lightbody, who had been recommended to the Edinburghs, as they were then known, by Princess Marina, and Miss Anderson were Scottish. Mabel, Eileen Parker remembered, 'was prim and proper' while Helen 'was an awfully kind person and terribly fair. Prince Charles adored her'. One of them, though no one knows who, serviced him with his earliest memory – of being pushed through Green Park in a pram, him at one end, his nanny's hands at the other, and wondering at the prodigious length of his carriage.

It was Nanny Lightbody – Charles called her 'Nana' – who got him up in the morning and dressed him, just as Allah had dressed Elizabeth. Nanny slept in the same room as him and comforted him if he woke during the night.

As Charles's step-grandmother-in-law, Dame Barbara Cartland, once observed, much of his early life was lived 'behind the green baize door... Mummy a remote and glamorous figure who came to kiss you goodnight, smelling of lavender and dressed for dinner. Prince Charles worshipped his mother, but from afar.' The habits Elizabeth had acquired in her own childhood were proving hard to break and, undemonstrative by nature, she always found it difficult to hug or kiss her son, preferring to leave such important tactile displays of emotion to the nannies.

Charles does not remember his mother kissing him at all after the age of eight. He wistfully told a girlfriend that his nanny meant more to him emotionally than his mother ever did.

Elizabeth became even more distant as a mother when George VI died and she became monarch. Godfrey Talbot, the BBC's Court Correspondent at the time, recalled: 'She had been trained since the cradle by her father that duty came before everything, including her family.

'She reluctantly had to abandon that family and they virtually didn't see their parents for months on end. It was very upsetting and bewildering for a little boy.'

In 1953 the new Queen and her consort left on a long-delayed tour of the Commonwealth. They were away for six months. Like her mother before her, Elizabeth cried at the parting. And as her mother had discovered after her six-month trip to Australia in 1927, the long absence exacted its inevitable toll.

When they were eventually reunited, the Queen recalled her children 'were terribly polite. I don't think they really knew who we were.'

OPPOSITE PAGE: Princess Elizabeth, Duchess of Edinburgh and the Duke of Edinburgh with their firstborn as he tries to grab his mother's pearls

BELLOW: The fair-haired, blue-eyed Prince, aged 19 weeks and weighing 16lb 2oz, is fascinated by a cuddly toy rabbit

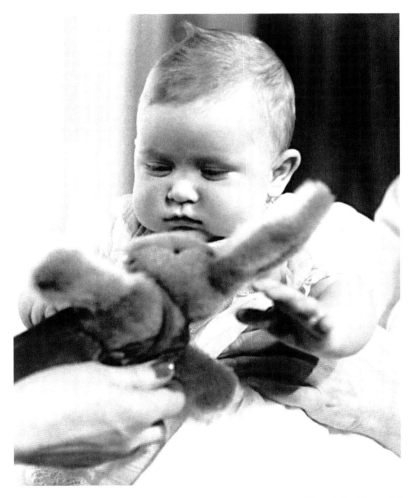

In Philip's case that was understandable. He had managed to spend Charles's first Christmas with his wife and son, but that would prove to be the last time for several years that they managed to be together for what is usually considered a time for family celebration. Charles's mother chose to leave her son at Sandringham with his grandparents and went to join her husband in Malta, where he was serving in the Royal Navy.

On Charles's third birthday his parents were away on a tour of North America.

Eileen Parker had known Philip for several years before he married the future Queen. From the very first, she said, 'He was a real loner. He was very good-looking; tall, with that blond hair and those piercing blue eyes.

'You would turn and say, "Who's that?" "Oh, that's Prince Philip of Greece, but he never has anything to do with anybody."'

Marriage had not mellowed him. He was a man of his time and background, just as his wife was a woman of hers. Very much a man's man, he enjoyed drinking and jesting with his cronies and continued to keep to a bachelor routine.

On one occasion he and Mike Parker were so late home to Clarence House, where he and his wife had established their first home, that he found the gates locked. He had to climb in over them. 'Serves them both right,' his wife commented dryly.

He was soon surrounded by a group of like-minded people his wife referred to as 'Philip's funny friends'. Mrs Parker thought them 'distinctly odd'.

The Palace old guard did not approve. They were concerned by what Eileen Parker saw as 'his apparent desire to continue bachelor friendships' with people of somewhat dubious reputation. But their attitude, rather than reining him back, only seemed to spur Philip on. Independent and single-minded, the Prince disliked the constraints imposed by his membership of the royal family.

In 1951 the ill-health of his father-in-law the King forced Philip to give up his active career in the Royal Navy, where he had excelled. When Elizabeth succeeded her father on the throne, he found himself outmanoeuvred by courtiers, who excluded him from having any say in his wife's affairs of state.

Even learning to fly a helicopter proved difficult. When the Prime Minister, Winston Churchill, learned that Philip had taken to the air, he summoned Mike Parker to Downing Street, kept him standing in silence for several minutes while he carried on working at his desk, then gave him 'a long accusing stare' and coldly asked, 'Is your objective the destruction of the whole of the royal family?'

Naturally irascible, such impositions served only to heighten Philip's irritation, as did the government's firm ruling, which had the backing of Queen Mary, that his children were not to be called Mountbatten, the surname he had assumed, but Windsor, as King George V had decreed. He felt, he complained, like a 'bloody amoeba'.

He had little time to devote to his son as he struggled to find a role for himself in these frustrating circumstances. Nor did he show any inclination to be a hands-on, nappy-changing kind of father. Charles, as everyone noted, was an 'exceptionally sweet-natured little boy' who was always thoughtful – of others and the world around him. He learned to walk with the help of a blue elephant on wheels called Jumbo, was soon fond of pedalling his tricycle down the corridors at Sandringham shouting 'Fire! Fire!' to the amusement of his grandparents, and was very attached to a stuffed rabbit, which he took to bed with him, and a teddy bear that would eventually accompany him to school.

LEFT: The happy Prince with his mother on his first birthday, 14 November 1949

OPPOSITE PAGE: Prince Richard of Gloucester keeps an eye on his cousin as they go for a walk in Green Park

King George VI, in his dying days, remarked, 'Charles is too sweet, stomping around the room.'

He was neither aggressive nor sporting, however; his little sister soon came to dominate him physically. He was not mechanically-minded like his father. He suffered from knock-knees like both his grandfather, George VI, and great-grandfather, George V. He had flat feet and had to wear a special pair of orthopaedic shoes. He was prone to chest complaints and a constant succession of coughs and throat ailments.

'Philip tolerated Charles but I don't think he was a loving father,' Eileen Parker observed. 'He would pick up Charles but his manner was cold. He had more fun with Anne. I think Charles was frightened of him.'

It is frequently stated – and generally believed – that Earl Mountbatten's overwhelming drive to succeed was motivated by his need to expunge the humiliation suffered by his father, whose German ancestry and accent forced his resignation as First Sea Lord at the outset of the First World War.

Philip also appeared to be compensating, subconsciously, for the failings of his father. Prince Andrew of Greece and Denmark had been accused of cowardice and condemned for treason. His son was a ruthlessly efficient naval officer who would have risen to very high rank had he been allowed to pursue his career. Those who knew Andrew during his exile in Paris remember him as an effeminate whinger. Philip, conversely, was overtly masculine and spoke his mind without apology. He set himself manly tasks and expected others to follow his example.

Philip believed in corporal punishment and Charles was summarily spanked if he was rude or obstreperous, though his father usually left the administration of such discipline to the nannies. His remarks, however, could be more wounding.

'He could be incredibly cutting, not only to his children, but to other people,' Mrs Parker recalled. ' He always had to fight for himself from the very beginning. The Queen adored him but she didn't rough it. He did rough it and I've heard him say some awful remarks.'

RIGHT: Nurse Mabel Anderson takes Charles for a second-birthday outing in London's St James's Park, 14 November 1950

OPPOSITE PAGE: The Prince looks into Queen Elizabeth's handbag with expectation after the christening of his sister at Buckingham Palace

The women charged with looking after the little boy did not always approve of the Duke's brusque methods. Just before the Queen and Philip embarked on their six-month tour, Catherine Peebles, another capable Scotswoman, was employed as governess. Charles, she recalled, was a reticent, reflective child.

'He liked being amused rather than amusing himself. He was very responsive to kindness but if you shouted at him he would draw back into his shell and you would be able to do nothing with him.' Philip's manner did not draw the best out of his son.

Nanny Lightbody also had her reservations. 'She never said she didn't like him but I don't think she saw eye to eye with him one bit,' said Mrs Parker. Philip's way of teaching his son to swim was to jump into the Buckingham Palace pool and loudly order the often terrified Charles in after him. One Saturday morning Charles was 'slightly chesty'. Nana did not want to let him into the water but Philip insisted. The little boy ended up with a bad cold. Nana was furious.

'I was very cross with his father,' she said later, 'but the trouble is I can only say so much.' Philip, still the naval officer at heart, did not tolerate his decisions being questioned.

Yet there were occasions when his manner would soften. And Mabel Anderson publicly insisted, 'He was a marvellous father. When the children were younger he always set aside time to read to them or help them put together those little model toys.'

Nonetheless, there were moments when his exasperation got the upper hand. He tried to teach his son to sail, without noticeable success. Charles was often seasick and did not respond well to the hearty discipline of a life onboard. He later recalled: 'I remember one disastrous day when we went racing and my father was, as usual, shouting. We wound the winch harder and the sail split in half with a sickening crack. Father was not pleased.

'Not long after that I was banned from the boat after an incident while cruising in Scotland. There was no wind and I was amusing myself taking pot shots at beer cans floating around the boat. The only gust of wind of the day blew the jib in front of my rifle just as I fired. I wasn't invited back onboard.'

The difference in their personalities opened a gulf between father and son. 'I didn't listen to advice from my father until I was in my late teens,' Charles said. He was more at ease in the company of his grandmother, who now bore the title Queen Elizabeth the Queen Mother.

As a mother she had been warm and loving but frequently distracted. Being a grandmother, however, suited her and she brought more affection to the role than Queen Mary had ever been capable of. In her dying days the old Queen unbent a little, allowing her great-grandson to play with her collection of jade objects, a pleasure she had sternly denied her granddaughters, Elizabeth and Margaret. But despite the mellowing sadness of old age (she lived to see her husband and three of her sons die and another exiled), she never lost her intimidating air of haughty majesty, even with her own family.

The new Queen Mother, by contrast, was gentle and welcoming.

She remembered her grandson as 'a very gentle boy with a very kind heart, which I think is the essence of everything'.

The feeling was reciprocated. On the occasion of her 80th birthday in 1980, Prince Charles said: 'Ever since I can remember, my grandmother has been the most wonderful example of fun, laughter, infinite security and, above all else, exquisite taste.

'For me, she has always been one of those extraordinarily rare people whose touch can turn everything into gold – whether it be putting people at their ease, turning something dull into something amusing, bringing happiness and comfort to people in her presence, or making any house she lives in a unique haven of cosiness and character. She belongs to that priceless brand of human beings whose greatest gift is to enhance life for others through her own effervescent enthusiasm for life.'

ABOVE: Charles, on Mabel Anderson's knee, and Anne, held by Helen Lightbody, leave Buckingham Palace for Sandringham, 22 December 1950

OPPOSITE PAGE: The Prince is at London Airport in April 1951 to greet Princess Elizabeth as she returns from Malta

The smartly-dressed second in line to the throne on 13 November 1951, the eve of his third birthday

The other grandmother was Philip's mother, Princess Alice, who had now retired into a nun's habit (the costume did not inhibit her chain-smoking consumption of noxious untipped Greek cigarettes or her taste for strong coffee and sherry). She made occasional visits to England from her convent retreat in Greece, and then spent the last years of her life at Buckingham Palace, where she died in 1969. She took particular delight in Charles's company, though he found her a rather alarming figure.

'She was very severe,' Eileen Parker remembered. 'She always sat bolt upright and had an almost overpowering personality. The room filled with smoke when she was around.' She spoke broken English in a thick, guttural accent. Because of her deafness she was hard to make conversation with. 'She had to be near you so that she could look at you and lip-read what you were saying,' Mrs Parker remembered. 'The Queen Mother was completely different. Very natural; she had the gift of putting you at your ease and making you feel as if you were the only person in the room.'

The Queen Mother once observed, 'I'm not as nice as you think I am.' Charles did not agree. She offered him a sanctuary from the 'near-Teutonic' demands of his father and a kindly embrace during the unavoidable absences of his mother.

'He turned to Granny for a shoulder to cry on,' Godfrey Talbot said. 'During the first years of the Queen's reign the Queen Mother was both mother and father.'

It was the nursery staff, though, who had the most direct influence on his young life. They taught him his manners. Particular emphasis was placed on politeness and he was taught from an early age to address people as 'Mr' or 'Mrs' and not to poke his tongue out or pull faces. Nanny Lightbody was forever saying, 'Have you said thank you?' and he was made to go and thank the engine driver whenever he took a train ride.

They protected him as best they could from his aggressive younger sister. They disciplined him when he was naughty, which was rarely. They made a home for him in the nursery and filled it with a menagerie of animals; as well as the corgis there were a pair of South American lovebirds named David and Annie (Mabel Anderson called them 'horrid, vicious creatures'), a hamster named Chi-Chi, and a rabbit called Harvey. The animals were a 'dominant passion' and Charles, taught to clean his own teeth, would try to brush Harvey's.

RIGHT: The Prince and his mother, by now Queen Elizabeth II, at Balmoral Castle in the summer of 1952

OPPOSITE PAGE: On his third birthday, Charles and Anne visit the King and Queen at Buckingham Palace. George VI's left lung was removed two months earlier

He developed an early interest in cooking and what went on in the palace kitchens and was forever popping in to help the chefs weigh out the ingredients, fetch the pots, and give warning when the saucepans and kettles were coming to the boil.

Not all his culinary efforts were successful. He was once sent to the storeroom by a chef named Aubrey – and dropped a tray loaded with butter, baking powder, two dozen eggs and sultanas on the floor on the way back. His attempts at making ice lollies were equally fraught. Mabel Anderson kept turning up the temperature of the nursery fridge because the milk was getting too cold. Charles kept turning it down again because his lollies wouldn't freeze. Whether it was the milk or the lollies that came out right depended on who had last been at the fridge. Not surprisingly, his presence did not always meet with the approval of the kitchen staff, who would complain that he got in the way.

He enjoyed ballroom and Scottish dancing and was taught, as his mother had been, by Miss Vacani who came to Buckingham Palace to give him lessons with a few children belonging to members of the Royal Household.

Miss Peebles said he had a strong sense of rhythm. Eileen Parker agreed and said, 'He was a very good dancer even at that young age and could keep time very well.' The Queen sometimes looked in to see how he was progressing.

The Queen and her children watch a Royal Air Force fly-past following her crowning at Westminster Abbey, 2 June 1953

OPPOSITE PAGE: Charles and his family return to London in February 1953 after their six-week holiday at Sandringham

The reserve Charles has never managed to overcome manifested itself from early on. As a little boy he found it difficult to mix with other children. He was very friendly with the Parkers' daughter Julie but, as her mother recalled, 'If there were other children there he would cling to Nanny Lightbody.' When he was nervous, Mrs Parker noted, his mouth would twitch to one side in the manner later seized on by comic impersonators.

That shyness carried through into his studies. Catherine Peebles, who was promptly named 'Mispy' as in 'Miss P', set up a schoolroom at Buckingham Palace, but instead of other children being invited to join him in his studies, as had then become the convention for children who were privately educated, Charles was taught on his own. Even his sister, Anne, was not allowed in when he was working.

As Arundel Herald Extraordinary, Dermot Morrah, noted in 1968 in his 'privileged account' of Charles's childhood 'written with the approval of HM The Queen', his mother 'saw that Charles was likely to get more embarrassment than encouragement from working as one of a group [an assessment Morrah considered correct], and consequently she decided that, at least while he was with Miss Peebles, he should have lessons alone.

'A good deal of what was important in his life was lived internally, within the bounds of his own imagination. Miss Peebles discovered that she had to deal with a vague child, or, perhaps more accurately, a child who still had only a vague relationship to the external world.' The doughty Mispy found herself dealing with a 'plodder' who was good at art but took rather a long time learning to read, found it hard to concentrate on written subjects and was incapable of understanding the 'language' of mathematics.

Like his mother before him, Charles was also taught to ride and swim (by the age of six) and taken on educational visits to the museums and, of greater interest, to Madame Tussauds, where he gazed at waxworks of the parents he saw less of than he would have wished. He also visited the London Planetarium, which fed his interest in the stars, an interest he shares with his mother, who is a 'country person' like himself.

RIGHT: Growing up fast, Prince Charles, Duke of Cornwall, sports a tie for his fifth-birthday portrait

OPPOSITE PAGE: Charles and Anne with the Mountbattens in Malta in April 1954 before meeting their parents on the new royal yacht in Tobruk

To ensure that these outings went off with the minimum of disruption, the Queen's press secretary, Commander Richard Colville, sent a letter to Fleet Street newspaper editors asking them to allow Charles to enjoy himself 'without the embarrassment of constant publicity'. It was a vain appeal. Attitudes towards the royal family had changed since the days when his mother could go for carriage rides around London waving politely to the people . In the still ordered society of the 1930s, royalty was treated with considerable deference. Twenty years later, public interest in this grand family, with its palaces and panoplies, had sharpened.

Royal-watching was becoming a national sport. The popular newspapers were pandering to their readers' interests, and when they discovered that Charles had started attending Hill House in Knightsbridge, a pre-prep school a few minutes' drive from the palace, a swarm of photographers and reporters descended.

The decision to break with royal tradition and send her son to a proper school illustrated the Queen's determination to give him a 'normal' childhood. This, she believed, was the best way to equip him for his future role as king, and in that she was encouraged by her husband.

'The Queen and I want Charles to go to school with other boys of his generation and learn to live with other children, and to absorb from childhood the discipline imposed by education with others,' Philip declared. The academic side was deemed to be of secondary importance. As Philip told his son, 'Look, I'm only going to bother if you're permanently bottom. I really couldn't care less where you are. Just stay in the middle, that's all I ask.' The middle was more or less where Charles stayed for the whole of his school life, except for mathematics where he was permanently rooted near the bottom.

That did not particularly concern his father. It was 'character' that he was interested in, and while it was the Queen who authorised this experiment in royal education, it was Philip who had the deciding say in which schools Charles would attend.

Hill House set the course. It was founded by Colonel Henry Townsend, a believer in the educational properties of sport and competition. His school tried to instil in its pupils, as its manifesto declared, 'a sense of rivalry… and the urge to win'. Both were new to the young Prince, surrounded as he had been by affectionate women – nannies, governess, his grandmother, his aunt Margaret – and only his sister to contend with.

RIGHT: Charles, wearing a kilt of Balmoral tartan, in the grounds of his mother's Aberdeenshire estate during the family's summer holiday in 1955

OPPOSITE PAGE: While a day pupil at Hill House school in Knightsbridge, central London, the eight-year-old Prince takes part in sports' day activities

Hill House was a day school and every evening he retreated to the security of home. At the age of eight, however, the boy who, as one of his biographers observed, 'had never been shopping… had never been on a bus… had never been lost in a crowd… had never had to fend for himself', was marched out of this supportive environment to follow in his father's footsteps, first to Cheam, then up to the remote coastal plain of Morayshire to Gordonstoun. He found the transition excruciatingly painful.

Charles's first few days as a boarder at Cheam, he would later recall, were the most miserable of his life, and his mother never forgot that he 'shuddered' with apprehension as he journeyed there for his first day.

'He dreaded going away to school,' Mabel Anderson recalled. 'He felt family separation very deeply.'

He would write to Mispy every day, Princess Anne recalled.

'He was heartbroken, he used to cry into his letters and say, "I miss you".' The governess was equally distressed by the absence of the little boy she had come to love. She stayed on to teach Anne and then Andrew, but her real interest was always Charles and they corresponded regularly for the rest of her life. Catherine Peebles died in the impersonal vastness of Buckingham Palace in 1968. She retired to her rooms one Friday night. No one missed her and her body was not found for 48 hours. Charles was inconsolable when told the news.

The Prince eventually settled in as best he could, but he did not have a particularly happy time there. He was too diffident, too shy to make friends easily or to stand out and up for himself in the rough and tumble. He still carried his puppy fat, and during one game of rugby was upset to hear the shout directed at him from somewhere below, 'Oh, get off me, Fatty!'

It was the same at Gordonstoun. Philip had thrived there. It did not suit his son. The hearty outdoor life, if never as Spartan as legend made out (there were always hot showers to go with the cold and the early-morning runs were little more than 50-yard trots up the road and then never when it was raining), was still tougher than he would have wished.

'I hated the institution, just as I hated leaving home,' he would later say. 'I did not enjoy school as much as I might have, but this was because I am happier at home than anywhere else.'

The American psychiatrist M. Scott Peck maintains that there is a 'pattern for children leaving home. Those who grew up in warm, nurturing, loving homes usually had relatively little difficulty in leaving those homes, while children who grew up in homes filled with back-biting, hostility, coldness and viciousness often had a great deal of trouble leaving.'

Author of the best-selling *The Road Less Traveled*, Peck continues: 'We tend to project on to the world what our childhood home is like. Children who grow up in nurturing homes tend to see the world as a warm and loving place and say, "Hey, let me at it." Children who grow up in a home filled with hostility and viciousness tend to see the world as a cold, hostile and dangerous place.'

Charles could certainly sense the hostility his regal position generated. He saw less of his mother than he would have liked and there were moments of tension with his father. And royal courts, even in a modern age, are breeding grounds for just the kind of backbiting hostilities to which Peck refers.

But whatever the flaws in his home life, Charles still enjoyed a full support system of nannies and female relations to service him with the necessary emotional succour which, had his temperament been of a different kind, might well have been enough to see him through. Anne confronted the outside world with vigorous self-confidence. Her brother did not.

'I had a dream,' he once recalled, 'that I was going to escape and hide in the forest, in a place where no one could find me, so I wouldn't have to go back to school.' More than anything he wanted to be with his grandmother, and Gordonstoun certainly stood in rugged contrast to that comforting, female-dominated world.

RIGHT: The 'C' on the Prince's cap is not for Charles but for Cheam, the Berkshire preparatory school he attended in the late 1950s

OPPOSITE PAGE: A whispered aside with Queen Elizabeth as the royal family pay their annual visit to the Braemar Gathering in September 1957

He was put into Windmill Lodge, whose housemaster, Robert Whitby, made a habit of appearing to be always angry and shouted a great deal. Another housemaster of that time described the school thus: 'Good for the very clever, good for the laird's idiot son, but not so good for the average boy.'

In matters academic and athletic Charles was never other than average. He only managed to pass O-level mathematics at the third attempt. His history, for all his stated view that 'I honestly believe that the only way one can hope to understand and cope with the present is by knowing and being able to interpret what happened in the past', was something of a struggle. On one well-reported occasion his tutor, Robin Birley, shouted at him in front of the whole class, 'Come on, Charles, you can do better than this – after all, this is the history of your family we're dealing with!' He was disappointing at rugby and cricket.

Where he did excel was in music and acting. He was taught to play the cello by an elderly German woman who had been at the school since Philip's day. And his ability on the stage was quickly noted by Dr Eric Anderson, who would go on to become headmaster of Eton. Anderson cast him in the role of Macbeth and he turned in a memorable performance. His artwork, and pottery in particular, was also of a high standard.

These were never more than very minor interests at a school that placed emphasis on the physical, however, and Charles often seemed out of step with his classmates. He had few friends amongst the school's 400 boys. He usually walked the half-mile from Windmill Lodge to lessons – in the complex of huts around the main school building – by himself. Those who tried to strike up a conversation with him had to endure a gauntlet of snide comments from their contemporaries, who would loudly accuse them of 'sucking up'.

The Queen Mother – aware of her grandson's introverted nature – had argued that he would be better served at Eton College, on the other side of the Thames from Windsor Castle, with its 600 years' experience of accommodating the wide-ranging interests of its pupils. A number of the Queen's advisors agreed with her. But Philip was not to be swayed and so Gordonstoun it was. In effect the decision meant an attempt to mould him in his father's image, to which 'he did not naturally approximate,' Dermot Morrah wrote.

Charles and Anne pull seven-month-old brother Andrew's pram at Balmoral in September 1960

OPPOSITE PAGE: In home-movie footage taken by the Queen in 1957, the siblings are buried up to their necks in sand on a Norfolk beach as a corgi stands guard

However, this did not prevent him becoming Guardian, as Gordonstoun's head boy is called, just as his father had been. The whole point of Charles's education was to train him to accept responsibility, a responsibility that was his by birthright and one that was not to be evaded.

'I didn't suddenly wake up in my pram one day and say, "Yippee",' he said, referring to the prospect of kingship, it just dawns on you slowly that people are interested… and slowly you get the idea that you have a certain duty and responsibility. It's one of those things you grow up in.'

His parents had tried to shield him from his fate for as long as possible. When he was three, for instance, a courtier passed him in one of the Buckingham Palace corridors.

'Where are you going?' the Prince asked.

'I'm going to see the Queen,' came the courtier's reply.

'Who's she?' Charles enquired.

In another break from tradition, he was not obliged to bow to his mother once she became queen. Reality could not be locked out for long, however, and he was soon well aware of his position. Soldiers presented arms when he passed them. Crowds cheered him when he drove by. And how many little boys have the band of the Grenadier Guards on call to play *The Teddy Bears' Picnic* for them on their birthday?

'You always felt he knew his destiny even at that age,' said Eileen Parker.

Charles was surrounded by reminders of who he was and what lay ahead. His mother's face was on the stamps he stuck on the letters to Mispy and on the coins he bought his chocolate with in the school tuck-shop – a fact that his pals at school were not slow to point out.

Brought up amongst the sons of the privileged, he was always more privileged. A police officer accompanied him to Gordonstoun. Whereas everyone else had to see each term at Gordonstoun through without the benefit of a break (there was no half-term holiday at the school when he was there), he was allowed out to join his parents on state occasions.

He was spared the anxiety of choosing a career: he was going to Cambridge. Then, and despite his seasickness, he was going into the Royal Navy. Earl Mountbatten spelled it out: 'Trinity College like his grandfather; Dartmouth like his father and grandfather; and then to sea in the Navy, ending up with a command of his own.' A suitable marriage would follow.

In 1987, in a cry of frustration, Charles declared: 'You can't understand what it's like to have your whole life mapped out for you a year in advance. It's so awful to be programmed. I know what I'll be doing next week, next month, even next year. At times I get so fed up with the whole idea.'

As a youth he had to bear it even if he couldn't grin. And no matter how definite the plan, it provided no protection against the bruisings he received along the way. Rather the contrary.

At Cheam he watched a TV programme in which his mother announced that she was going to make him Prince of Wales.

'I remember being acutely embarrassed,' he recalled. 'I think for a little boy of nine it was rather bewildering. All the others turned and looked at me in amazement.'

He was faced with similar moments throughout his schooldays. His photograph was often in the newspapers, and if the accompanying stories owed more to imagination than fact, that was no consolation to Charles as he struggled and usually failed to live up to the image the press were determined to create for him.

One small example was an article that appeared in the *Daily Express* when he was at Gordonstoun. The William Hickey column boldly predicted that the 'Action Man' Prince would make the rugby 1st XV. That caused considerable mirth amongst pupils and sports masters alike, for Charles never even made the 4th, the lowest team fielded by the school.

Such incidents left their mark. He could be gracious and charming. When faced with situations over which he had no control, however, he would withdraw deep into himself. Fearful of confrontation, desperate to avoid ridicule, he constructed a wall of regal reserve to protect the sensitivity which had been his most notable characteristic as a child.

ABOVE: The Prince of Wales, now in his 12th year, is driven from Buckingham Palace to see his grandmother at Clarence House in February 1960

OPPOSITE PAGE: Queen Elizabeth II and her heir out riding in the grounds of Windsor Castle in May 1961

Anne

PRINCESS ANNE ONCE observed that she should have been a boy. There are those who are close to the royal family who believe that she should not only have been born a boy but that she should also have been the eldest. Prince Philip is one who held that view.

She is gutsy, sensible and pragmatic. She does not talk to plants. She is not given to bouts of introspection. She is single-minded and believes in deeds, not words. She is sporty and brave. She is unimpressed by rank or title, is unafraid of controversy and cares little for the opinion of others.

And if she can be disconcertingly royal when the mood takes her ('I'm not your "love". I'm your Royal Highness', she once admonished an over-familiar photographer), she is someone who has no qualms about letting her hair down and mucking in when the occasion so demands.

In other words, she is very much her father's daughter in a way that Charles could never be his father's son. Of all his children, Anne is the only one who merits a photograph in his private office at Buckingham Palace.

'He always had more fun with Anne,' Eileen Parker observed. 'Charles is more like the Queen while Anne is very like Prince Philip.'

The Duke of Edinburgh would later admit: 'Perhaps I did spoil her at times.'

Anne was born on 15 August 1950. 'It's the sweetest girl,' Philip remarked. 'With quite a definite nose for one so young,' photographer Cecil Beaton cattily observed). She was 21 months younger and, at 6lb, was 1lb 6oz lighter than her brother. What she gave away in weight and age she soon made up for in temper and physical determination.

'Anne would boss Charles; she would take command of things,' recalled Mrs Parker. 'If she saw a toy she wanted, she would grab it. She grabbed everything that Charles wanted, and everything he had wanted.'

Charles had a blue pedal car he was particularly fond of. He was often unceremoniously bundled out of it by his more aggressive sister. It was the same with the tricycle they shared. If Charles was riding it, Anne was sure to want it.

'There were terrible scenes,' said Mrs Parker, who used to entertain the royal siblings at her home in Launceston Place, Kensington. 'Nanny Lightbody would say, "Now stop this!"'

There was no stopping Anne, however. When their father presented them each with a pair of boxing gloves and tried to instruct them in the art of self-defence they set about each other with such fury that he had to take the gloves away again.

Once, when they were at Balmoral, Lady Adeane, the wife of the Queen's private secretary, gave them a paper bag full of mushrooms she had just picked. A row quickly ensued over who was going to present them to their mother.

They started tugging at the bag, which burst open, spilling its contents over the gravel drive – at which point Anne, who had just returned from a riding lesson, set about her brother with her riding crop.

Charles burst into tears just as the Queen opened the door. In exasperation, she shouted: 'Why can't you behave yourselves?' and boxed them both around the ears.

As the Princess herself later admitted: 'We fought like cat and dog.'

'No' was not a word she readily responded to. 'When she got really worked up she would start throwing things at him,' Mrs Parker said. 'She was very strong-willed, a real menace.'

Anne was forever ignoring her nanny's instructions not to take too many toys out, instead emptying the entire cupboard on to the floor and, in those days of coal fires in every room, making herself filthy in the process.

OPPOSITE PAGE: Princess Anne wears her coronation dress of cream lace over chiffon and taffeta for a photograph to mark her third birthday

If she didn't get her way 'she had the most frightful fit of temper, lying on the floor and kicking with sheer temper'.

Charles was surprisingly nice to his boisterous little sister ('perhaps too nice,' Mrs Parker thought), always inviting her to join in his games, taking a concerned and conciliatory attitude towards her excesses. For all their squabbles, the two got on reasonably well together. They had to. For like their mother and her sister before them, Charles and Anne spent more of their infancy in the company of adults – servants, courtiers, family members – than they did with children of their own age and it was to each other that they turned for playful companionship.

That happened to suit Charles, who did not mix easily. Conversely, Anne was 'always very confident,' Mrs Parker noted.

At Madame Vacani's dance classes, Charles would hang back, clutching on to nanny and watching as Anne 'would go off with other children'. While Charles was often too shy to chat, 'Anne talked non-stop'.

She was also much naughtier than her compliant brother. She was the one who kicked the corgis. During her days as a Brownie she set off a major alert when she disappeared into a bush in the palace grounds and started frantically blowing her whistle. That brought a posse of policemen, uniformed and plain-clothed, courtiers, gardeners and Guardsmen running to the scene – much to her mischievous delight.

It was Anne who teased the sentries on duty. As soon as she discovered that they presented arms whenever she walked past them, she started doing just that, much to the anger of Nanny Lightbody.

RIGHT: The Edinburghs and children in their private sitting room at Clarence House, January 1951

OPPOSITE PAGE: Queen Mary attends Princess Anne's christening at Buckingham Palace on 21 October 1950

Charles was never so daring; he had confined himself to imitating their march.

But if Anne was more than her brother's equal on the parade ground of the palace forecourt or the battlefield of the nursery, it was Charles who commanded the greatest attention, no matter what their father might think about his abilities. He was born to be king and that fact was subtly drummed into him and his sister from earliest memory.

By her own account Anne 'always accepted the role of being second in everything from quite an early age. You adopt that position as part of your experience. You start off in life very much a tail-end Charlie, at the back of the line.'

However much the Princess might kick and scream, there, by genetic accident and the law of primogeniture, was she destined to remain.

She would be grateful for that in years to come. She developed a healthy view of her position in the royal hierarchy.

'I'm the Queen's daughter and as a daughter I get less involved than the boys,' she said.

That allowed her to develop her own interests, in her own way, without the pressures of a centre-stage royal role that so inhibited Charles.

'I'm me, I'm a person, I'm an individual, and I think it's better for everybody that I shouldn't pretend to be anything that I'm not,' she once remarked. If the public really wanted a 'Fairy Princess' to fill a void, then the Princess of Wales was much better suited to the part, she caustically observed.

She was not quite so self-effacing as a youngster. As her authorised biographer, Brian Hoey, noted: 'Perhaps it was this feeling of being second all the time that subconsciously prompted her as a young child to push her way to the front whenever she and Prince Charles were together. If he held back when she appeared in public, Princess Anne would be first out of the car or train, determined that no one would miss her.'

There was no place for her, though, at the coronation of her mother. She was too young to witness that pivotal transition

not just from one reign to the next, but from one era to another – from an age where the monarchy was secure in its position to one in which it would be thrown into stark relief and, within 40 years, see its value and continued existence called into question.

George VI died at his beloved Sandringham on 6 February 1952. Of equal import was the death 13 months later of his mother, Queen Mary. Grand and imperious, she had insisted on her due respect to the very end. Charles and Anne were ordered to bow and curtsey when they came into her presence.

But if she was the epitome of patrician rectitude, she was also a sad figure burdened by longevity – a queen consort whose Empire was in terminal decline and whose heirs would come to shed, through force of circumstance but also through vagaries of temperament, much of the awesome majesty she had stoutly believed was essential to the monarchy. Anne often stubbornly refused to curtsey to her great-grandmother.

Queen Mary's death in March 1953 should have delayed the Coronation. By the old-fashioned protocol of which she was the ultimate symbol, the court should still have been in mourning on 2 June 1953 when Elizabeth was crowned in Westminster Abbey.

But in a last gesture to the formality that had governed her life, Queen Mary left instructions that the Coronation should go ahead as scheduled. It did, with all the pomp and ceremony that Edward VII and his advisors had been able to devise.

Indeed, so recent was the pageantry revamped that when the procedure for the Queen's accession was discussed, Crown Equerry Sir Norman Gwatkin said, 'Let's look at an old copy of *Illustrated London News* and see what they did last time.'

Charles – aged four and a half but technically senior royal duke and head of the peerage – was taken in at the last minute to see his mother crowned. He was brought in at the back to stand between the Queen Mother and Princess Margaret. He was dressed in a cream satin suit. His nanny said, 'I just hope everything goes all right, as you know what children are.'

Midway through the ceremony he wiped his hair and put his hands to his nose – Nanny Lightbody had combed his hair down with his father's brilliantine and he wanted to smell it.

Princess Anne, not quite three, remained at Buckingham Palace, suffering 'the normal sisterly fury at being left behind'. There was a party for all the children in the Madame Vacani dancing class. They watched the ceremony on a flickering black and white television set. It was also the day that the news came through that Edmund Hillary had conquered Everest.

'My husband and Prince Philip were more interested in watching that than going to the Coronation,' Eileen Parker recalled vividly.

Princess Anne's memories of the day itself are inevitably vague. What she does remember is being taken out on to the balcony afterwards with the rest of the family and being told to wave to the people.

It was a public lesson in the demands that came with being a princess. There was no escape from being royal. As she would later say, 'The idea of opting out is a non-starter.'

BELOW: Anne and Charles have fun at Balmoral during their 1952 summer holiday. The Princess celebrated her second birthday whilst there

OPPOSITE PAGE: Princess Elizabeth and the Duke of Edinburgh with the children in the garden at Clarence House in August 1951

In the 1950s there were nonetheless long periods when the British royal family were able to enjoy the privilege of comparative anonymity. Anne's childhood, she recalled, was mercifully spared the unremitting attention that befell the next generation.

'The pattern of my life from birth until I went to boarding school at the age of 13 was living in London during the week and at Windsor at the weekends,' she wrote.

'The holidays were divided between Christmas and the New Year at Sandringham, Easter at Windsor and most of the summer at Balmoral.'

Anne settled into the time-honoured routine of country life. Schoolwork would occasionally intrude, and to help improve their French a tutor, a certain Mademoiselle de Roujoux, was employed. But football seemed to play as important a part in the curriculum as irregular verbs.

'The Queen is goalkeeper and Prince Philip, Princess Margaret and the children join in,' recalled Mademoiselle de Roujoux.

'Charles and Anne were little devils and never stopped playing tricks on me. The last words they shouted at me as I left for the train home were "*Café au lait, au lit*", which I had taught them and which they had found most amusing. It means, "coffee with milk in bed".'

It was a pastorale of advantaged youth. Anne learned to ride on a strawberry roan pony named William. She had the pleasure of threshing the corn and witnessing the corgis' 'inefficient attempts to kill the rats that ran out from the shrinking stacks', and watching the passage of the seasons in an age before advancements in agricultural machinery and methods changed the countryside for ever.

In Scotland there was 'the magic of the views of Lochnagar and the Dee valley, the beautiful autumn colours of the rowans and silver birches, the majesty of the Caledonian Forest and the animals and birds that live in these relatively unspoilt wild places'. At Sandringham there was 'the best riding country' across miles of flat stubble fields on the family estate.

'In the early Fifties, when I was growing up, there were still lots of people working and living in the countryside,' the Princess recalled. 'Information was passed from parents to children; knowledge was absorbed rather than taught. My "knowledge" of ponies, horses and riding was acquired that way, by absorption.'

The Queen took an active interest in Charles and Anne's equestrian progress and would go out with them whenever she could. 'I really don't know how she put up with the noise and aggravation that almost always seemed unavoidable whenever my brother and I did anything together.'

It was Anne's father, however, who encouraged her riding. When he saw how good she was – and how much better than her brother – he contacted Sir John Miller, then Crown Equerry, and told him to 'get on with it'.

'Not being nearly as brave as my sister – which very often happens – I rather got put off,' Charles recalled. While he was still at the end of a leading rein, Anne was jumping and galloping before she had properly learned how to trot. The Duke of Edinburgh had no reservations about letting his daughter expose herself to the dangers inherent in equestrian sport. 'It was almost as if he treated her as a son,' one observer recalled.

Philip was not the most attentive of fathers. He had been promoted to the rank of lieutenant-commander in the Royal Navy on the day Anne was born and given command of his own ship, the frigate HMS *Magpie*. He had helped choose her names and Anne – which King George V had overruled in the case of Princess Margaret – finally made it into the royal nomenclature.

Philip registered her with Westminster Food Office and obtained for her a ration book, number MAPM/36, that the little Princess, like the rest of the population in the austere post-war years, still required in order to obtain her allowance of meat, eggs, butter, bread, sugar, milk and, for a growing child, a weekly bottle each of orange juice and cod liver oil.

The Duke flew home from Malta where he was stationed for the christening, which was held in the Music Room of Buckingham Palace. The godparents were the Princess's grandmothers, Queen Elizabeth and Princess Andrew of Greece; Prince Philip's eldest sister, Princess Margarita of Hohenlohe-Langenburg; Andrew Elphinstone, the Queen's cousin; and Earl Mountbatten).

After that Philip very much went his own way. Even when he had to give up his naval career to devote his considerable energy to mounting royal duties, he was as likely to spend his evenings out with his cronies as at home with his family.

One of his friends was Prince Alfonso von Hohenlohe, the founder of the Marbella Club, who would scandalise European society by marrying Princess Ira von Fürstenberg, the heiress to the Agnelli car fortune, who was still only 15 at the time.

Prince Philip did find the time, though, to introduce his daughter to sailing on the waters of Loch Muick near Balmoral with considerably more success than he had with Charles. Anne soon became a proficient yachtswoman.

He would also take them camping on the windblown Highland hills. They would cook their bacon, sausages and eggs, brew tea and then spend the night in sleeping bags in a bothy built in Queen Victoria's day as a picnic hut.

Again it was Anne rather than her altogether more delicate brother who derived the greater pleasure from these Spartan escapades. But that, given their physical differences, was inevitable. Charles was a poor athlete; Anne became a first-class tennis and lacrosse player and, most notably, an Olympic three-day-event rider.

The contrast was reflected in their relationships with their parents. Charles gravitated towards his mother, who provided him with a sympathetic ear; Anne was close to Philip. Charles sometimes gave the impression of being terrified of his father, who seemingly had little understanding of his son's tears and inhibitions and was inclined to laugh at them.

He laughed at Anne too, but she could deal with that, cheerfully braving his ridicule, saying anything she wanted to him, and laughing back at him and with him, as she did when they were playing a game involving car numberplates.

LEFT: Princess Anne and her brother, the Duke of Cornwall, in the outfits they wore for their mother's coronation

OPPOSITE PAGE: The somewhat overwhelmed siblings with their parents on the balcony of Buckingham Palace, 2 June 1953

To keep his children amused on car journeys, Philip would call out the registrations of passing vehicles and ask them to make a sentence out of the letters. One car had the number plate PMD.

'That's easy,' Anne said. 'Philip's my dad!'

In the comparison with Anne, Charles did not even have the compensation of a shining academic lead. Anne was intelligent and capable of passing examinations with ease. Her eventual A-level grades in history and geography would have been sufficient to secure her a university place if she had wanted one, which she didn't.

'I think it's an overrated pastime,' she said, articulating her family's anti-intellectual bias.

Neither the Queen nor Prince Philip took a particular interest in Anne's academic progress. Before she was sent away to Benenden, a very Establishment girls' boarding school in Kent, she had been educated privately at Buckingham Palace under the tutelage of Miss Peebles.

The schoolroom was in the old nursery wing. The Queen's rooms were close by on the floor below. Yet Princess Anne has no recollection of her mother paying even one visit to see how she was progressing.

It was left to Princess Margaret to monitor her niece's work, and she did so with enthusiasm, going into the schoolroom to speak with the governess and conducting oral examinations of her own.

It was the foundation of a relationship between aunt and niece that matured into adult friendship, even though the results of these impromptu tests were not always as satisfactory as 'Charlie's Aunt', as Margaret called herself, might have wished.

Although Miss Peebles was a competent enough teacher, Charles had been her favourite and when he left to go to Cheam she 'virtually lost interest', Anne recollected. She didn't go to any lengths to hide her

belief that after Charles everyone else was second best. There was never any overt estrangement between the governess and her pupil, but when Mispy died Anne did not share her brother's sense of bereavement. In fact, she felt no emotion at all except guilt. That, she said, was only brought on precisely because she didn't feel any sense of loss.

Anne had been as upset as Miss Peebles when Charles left for his first boarding school. Despite their arguments, brother and sister were always close. It was to offset her sense of loneliness that two girls of her own age were invited to join her for lessons at Buckingham Palace. They were Susan Babington-Smith, granddaughter of an admiral who had been equerry to George V, and Caroline Hamilton, granddaughter of the Dean of Windsor.

According to Susan, who married John Hemming, director of the National Geographic Society, all three were treated in exactly the same way.

If there was any favouritism it worked against Anne. 'There was the odd time when Miss Peebles would be stricter with her than she was with us,' she recalled.

BELOW: Princess Anne gets a helping hand from a police officer as she alights from a car at the Marsa polo grounds in Malta on 5 May 1954

She and Prince Charles arrive at Aberdeen railway station early in the morning of 23 May 1954 after travelling overnight from London

OPPOSITE PAGE: Anne wheels her barrow as Charles cuddles up to the Queen Mother in the garden at Royal Lodge, April 1954

There was never any doubt, though, about who was royal. 'Not by anything she consciously did or said,' Mrs Hemming said. 'It was simply something about her that made us realise that she was different.'

They could hardly fail to miss the clues. Their classroom was in Buckingham Palace. At 11.30am every day the military band in the forecourt would strike up for the Changing of the Guard. Celebrity visitors like Soviet cosmonaut Yuri Gagarin called by. And, if there were still any doubt, on state occasions the governess would break off lessons and take the three girls to a window to watch the carriages depart. The Queen, in crown and full regalia, would look up and give a wave. Philip, in his Admiral of the Fleet uniform (a promotion directly related to his marriage) would blow them a kiss.

There were also Princess Anne's own outings to emphasise the difference in their status. She was a bridesmaid at the weddings of Earl Mountbatten's daughter, Lady Pamela, to interior designer David Hicks; Princess Margaret to society photographer Antony Armstrong-Jones; and the Duke of Kent to Katharine Worsley.

When her brother Andrew was born, as well as pushing him around the garden in his pram, she also appeared in the official photographs. And when her two friends were invited to join the Princess at Wimbledon, they watched the tennis from the royal box.

It was an idealised, hugely privileged style of education, and in any previous generation it would have continued to its conclusion. Philip had other ideas.

As with Charles, he wanted Anne to see life on the other side of the palace walls. It was, he argued, a vital preparation for dealing with the exigencies of the modern world. Benenden, a traditional establishment for 'young ladies', was chosen. At the age of 13 Anne became not the first Princess to be sent away to school (that was Alexandra, the Queen's cousin), but the first daughter of a reigning sovereign.

Like Charles, she was stricken with nerves on her first day and was physically sick on her way to the school. Unlike Charles, she soon settled in and did well. Anne's first impression of school was the 'continuous noise and the fact that everywhere you turned there were so many people'.

Any adjustment problems she may have had she kept to herself. She was not, so her contemporaries noted, a 'whiner' and the headmistress only learned of her bout of nausea *en route* to the school by chance, and then not until several weeks later.

RIGHT: The Queen and her daughter adjust the bridle on Greensleeves, the Princess's pony, at Balmoral in 1955

OPPOSITE PAGE: Anne, Charles and grandmother Princess Alice arrive in Portsmouth for a cruise on *Britannia*

Princess Anne was put in Magnolia dormitory with three other girls, and had drummed into her the oldest rule of the British public school system: to learn how to command one must first learn how to serve.

She waited on table and was made to give up her seat to girls her senior, and follow the routines and traditions of an establishment of which she was a very small part.

She learned how to handle money, a commodity the royal family have very little practical experience of.

'We had £2 a term and as I had been brought up by a careful Scots nanny to appreciate the value of money, I simply didn't spend my allotment. I've always been mean with money and, as far as I know, I was the only girl in the school who had any left by the end of term.'

The Princess was encouraged to pursue her riding at the nearby Moat House equestrian school run by Mrs Hatton-Hall, who, as Cherry Kendall, had been a top class three-day-eventer.

Anne eventually rose to be a prefect and captain of her house. She was, the headmistress Miss Elizabeth Clarke noted, 'able to exert her authority in a natural manner without being aggressive'.

She then added the criticism that would always be levelled against her most famous pupil: 'If there was any failing it was possibly her impatience.

'She was extremely quick to grasp things herself and couldn't understand anyone else not being able to do so.'

Anne's own memories of her time at Benenden are pleasant ones. 'I enjoyed my time at school, and no doubt my riding experiences helped', she wrote.

Her willingness not to stand on royal ceremony had certainly helped.

She was, as she said, determined to be herself and be judged by that criterion. Children, she later observed, 'accept people for what they are rather quicker than adults do. They have no preconceived ideas.'

Prince Charles, who was never allowed to forget who he was, would not have agreed, but then he was very different in character from his sister, who had the independence of mind to stand up for herself and even went so far as to admit: 'As a child and up to my teens, I don't think I went along with the family bit.'

Yet however determined she was to go her own way, she was never allowed to forget her royal status. As a concession to her position she was allowed out to attend certain state ceremonies though they were severely rationed because, as Elizabeth Clarke observed, 'The creation of precedents has to be watched in school life.'

BELOW: Horse-mad Princess Anne with Greensleeves in the Home Park at Windsor for a ninth-birthday portrait

The Princess, with Lady Rupert Nevill as her passenger, takes a turn behind the wheel of a dodgem car at a funfair in London in 1959

OPPOSITE PAGE: Three generations of royal ladies brave the cold at a meet of the West Norfolk Foxhounds in January 1958

There were other, more insidious reminders of who she was and what was expected of her. As a child, her parents had 'warned me that some people would want to make friends because of who you are. And I think that was fair comment, and it was important to know that.'

Even children who, as Anne would have it, accepted her for what and not who she was, were kept at arms' length. When Anne left for Benenden, all contact with Susan Babington-Smith and Caroline Hamilton ended.

'We never wrote to each other after leaving the palace,' Susan said. 'We didn't even have a farewell party. There was no contact. It was just the end of one part of one's life and the beginning of the next.'

Susan believed that the unnatural parting was part of an official policy. 'I'm sure it was laid down by the Queen and her advisors that we should split up,' she said.

The Queen and Prince Philip had broken with tradition by sending Charles and Anne away to school. The change was only intended to go so far. They were still 'royal', the glass wall still in place. Charles would retreat behind it.

When it came to raising a family of her own, Anne, like her aunt Margaret, would do what she could to shatter it.

BELOW: Anne and Sandra Butter are among the bridesmaids at the wedding of Katharine Worsley to the Duke of Kent at York Minster on 8 June 1961

The 12-year-old Princess in the uniform of the 1st Buckingham Palace Company of Girl Guides, August 1963

OPPOSITE PAGE: Anne and baby Andrew visit Queen Elizabeth the Queen Mother at Clarence House on her 60th birthday, 4 August 1960

The Queen with four-year-old Andrew and baby Edward at Buckingham Palace in June 1964

Andrew & Edward

NANNY MABEL ANDERSON used to remark that no nursery could hold two Prince Andrews. Yet however naughty he was – and he could be very naughty indeed – Mabel loved him dearly. Enough to pick up the telephone 30 years later and tearfully ask him if what she had just heard on the radio was really true – that he and his duchess were about to separate.

When Andrew heard his old nanny's voice he covered the receiver, turned to his wife and asked with a trembling voice, 'What shall we say to Mabel?'

Fergie, faced with her own problems and depressed by what she regarded as Andrew's inability to measure up as a husband, replied: 'Tell her what you want.'

Mabel Anderson was distraught to think of her beloved Andrew's unhappiness. Rejection was not something he had been trained to deal with. The cosy nursery world his nanny had created for him three decades earlier before had in no way prepared him for the emotional upheaval he was now experiencing. Mabel, by then in her late sixties, was aware of this and she was worried. So was Andrew.

It was a very long way from the Buckingham Palace days, which Mabel remembered so fondly.

Andrew was born on the afternoon of 19 February 1960, the first child to be born to a reigning British monarch in 103 years. The Queen and Prince Philip had been married for twelve and a half years.

The unplanned pregnancy came on the eve of a Canadian tour that was scheduled to cover 16,000 miles in nine weeks. It was a taxing journey for a woman in the early stages of pregnancy, but the Queen ignored any advice. Unlike her sister, Margaret, she seldom drank, had never smoked and was, she insisted, in the best of health.

The strain of the intervening years had taken their toll, and the hormonal changes the Queen was experiencing left her very tired. But she refused to give in and rest and, stubborn to the last, she came home from the tour exhausted and was immediately ordered to bed by her surgeon-gynaecologist, Lord Evans. Five days later she had recovered sufficiently to journey to Balmoral for the summer.

The beginning of the 1960s was a time of great change, not least for the monarchy. Recent years had seen rumours as to the state of Elizabeth and Philip's marriage, and during 1959 the royal family had come under attack, as their relevance began to be questioned for the first time in a debate started by Lord Altrincham, the writer John Grigg, who later renounced his peerage.

The announcement of the 7lb 3oz infant Prince's arrival, however, was greeted with the usual patriotic fervour the British reserve for royal births. There was much rejoicing amongst the crowd in The Mall, who were treated to a fly-past of 36 Hunter jets over Buckingham Palace and the traditional 21-gun salute.

Inside the palace, Prince Philip was in his study, far away from the bathroom of the Belgian Suite on the ground floor that had been converted into a delivery room. His wife had made it clear she didn't want him hanging around – and certainly not at her side for the birth.

That idea was distasteful to her. She was far happier to be in the care of her medical team, headed by Lord Evans, John Peel – later Sir John Peel, who spent the night in a nearby room – and midwife Sister Rowe.

It was Lord Evans who told the Duke that the waiting was over, that his wife had given birth to a son. As soon as Philip heard the news he ran out of his study, taking the stairs two at a time, and burst into the bedroom of the Belgian Suite.

He took his newborn gingerly from the nurse and held him in his arms. On his wife's previous instructions his first call was to the Queen Mother and Princess Margaret.

He then bounded upstairs again to the nursery to tell Princess Anne she had a baby brother. 'It's a boy!' he shouted excitedly to the nursery staff.

The birth of a royal baby is a cause for celebration among the palace staff. By tradition a bottle of fine vintage port is sent to each department 'to drink a toast with Her Majesty'. In some departments the port is raffled, and one lucky footman won a special bottle after the births of both Prince Andrew and Prince Edward. The port had been a gift to the Queen from the President of Portugal.

Andrew asserted himself from the moment of his birth, crying lustily when hungry until he got some attention. On the advice of her doctors the Queen was encouraged to breastfeed the baby for the first weeks before switching to the bottle. She was helped by Sister Rowe who, acting as a maternity nurse, was on call to bring the baby from his canopied cot in the nursery to his mother's bedroom.

LEFT: Prince Andrew in the arms of his grandmother, Queen Elizabeth the Queen Mother, in the garden of Clarence House, 4 August 1960

OPPOSITE PAGE: Laughing Andrew sits up in his pram at Balmoral in September 1960 as he holds his father's and sister's fingers

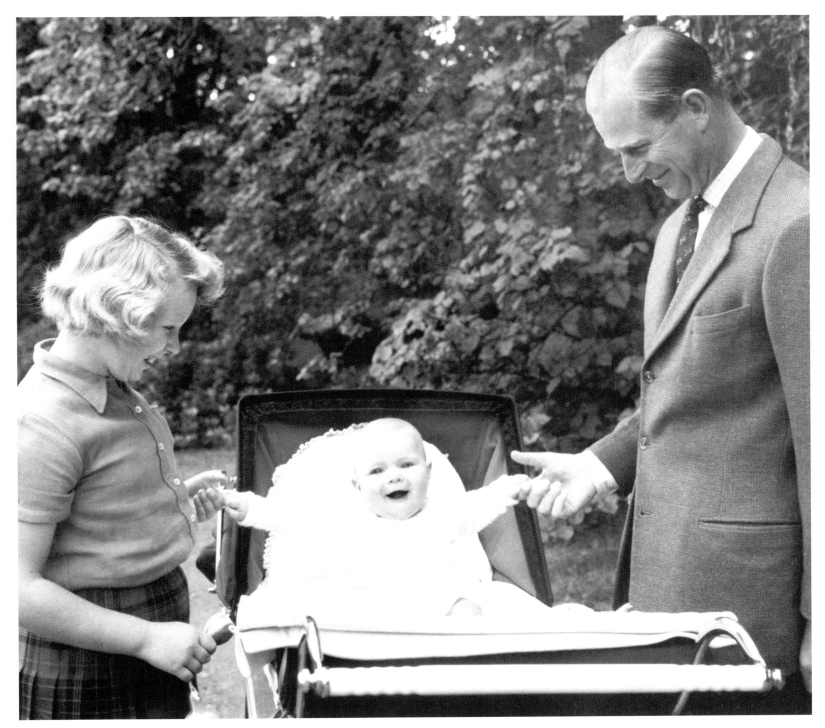

The Queen and Sister Rowe were great believers in the benefits of fresh air, and unless it was foggy or raining Andrew would sleep in the palace garden for a couple of hours each day in a large Silver Cross pram.

Sometimes the Queen would push the pram around the garden when she took the corgis for their afternoon walk. She was determined to enjoy motherhood to what she considered its fullest extent, which was not very much by ordinary standards, but more than she had been able to give to either Charles or Anne.

This did not run to changing nappies and nightly bathing of the baby, but it did mean she allotted him as much time as her role as monarch allowed.

In her typically orderly way, the Queen pencilled into her leather-bound appointment book the times she would be with Andrew. And during that time, nothing short of a crisis would prevent her from being with her baby. It was a lesson she had learnt when, as a young monarch with two small children, affairs of state had had to take precedence.

A few days before Andrew's birth, a statement was issued by Buckingham Palace declaring that the Queen's children would henceforth use the surname Mountbatten-Windsor – a combination of Philip's adopted name of Mountbatten and hers of Windsor.

It was in clear defiance of the promise she had given in council in 1952, but the Queen was now eight years into her reign, and was experienced and confident enough to do things her way.

Andrew Albert Christian Edward became the first royal child to hold the new family name from birth. He was christened in the Music Room at Buckingham Palace on 8 April 1960.

He was also the first royal child not to have official christening photographs. Instead, his father snapped away with his Hasselblad camera as the godparents (or sponsors as they are known in royal circles) stood around the silver lily font. Prince Henry, Duke of Gloucester; Princess Alexandra; Lord Elphinstone; the Earl of Euston; and Mrs Harold Phillips were the honoured friends and relatives chosen.

Philip and the Queen were of the opinion that Charles and Anne had suffered unnecessarily from over-zealous media attention during their formative years – especially Charles, who was painfully shy. They

The Queen, in uniform after the 1961 Birthday Parade, and her second son on the balcony at Buckingham Palace

OPPOSITE PAGE: Her Majesty and her two youngest children pose for photographer Cecil Beaton in June 1964

decided the best way of avoiding a repetition of the situation was to keep the baby, second in line to the throne, away from public places. Instead of going to the park, Nanny would restrict walks to the gardens of Buckingham Palace and Windsor Castle, well away from any public highway. That way the media coverage the baby received could be controlled.

The first photographs of Prince Andrew to be released were those taken by Cecil Beaton, when the baby was already one month old. Beaton's diaries give a revealing and acerbic account of the event, which the photographer clearly did not enjoy one bit.

'We were set for action when my friend Sister Rowe arrived with the baby who was kept quiet with a bottle,' Beaton noted.

'The baby, thank God, behaved itself and did not cry or spew. It sometimes opened its eyes. But even so I felt the odds tremendously against me. The weight of the Palace crushed me. The Queen seemed affable enough but showed no signs of real interest in anything... Not one word of conversation – only a little well-bred amusement at the way I gave my instructions in a stream of asides [to his assistant].

'P. Philip in that maddening Royal way kept suggesting I should use a ladder – take it from here – why not there – once I told him why not and quite firmly.'

Much to Beaton's relief, Philip started taking photographs of his own 'with a camera that had a lens three times the size of mine'.

With Philip distracted, Beaton tried to get a suitable picture. 'The baby was good. Sister Rowe was good – and I felt that the poor little Prince Charles was good... I realised soon that he was nice and kind and sensitive – but he has to be hearty – to be in a perpetual rugger scrum because that's what Papa expects of him. Somehow from his bright blue eyes – and sweet smile, I got more sympathy from him than any of the others...

'As it was, it was Prince Philip who called the whole thing off. As he loaded his camera anew he kept saying over his shoulder "surely we've had enough – if he's not got what he wants by now he's an even worse photographer than I think he is!" Ha! Hah! That sort of joke is admirable for the Mess or an official review – but oh the boredom of today.'

This extract clearly reveals both the photographer's dislike of Prince Philip and the Queen's painful shyness. Even holding her new baby and surrounded by family she felt uncomfortable in the presence of strangers although she had known Beaton since the 1940s when he first photographed her and Princess Margaret. Being photographed is not something the royal family ever enjoys. As Andrew, who became a keen

photographer himself, later observed, 'My family cringe when they hear the sound of a motor-drive, even if it's mine.'

Martin Charteris decided no further photographs would be released until the Queen Mother's 60th birthday on 4 August, and only then because Queen Elizabeth herself suggested that it might be nice to have the baby in the pictures too.

The lack of any real news or meaningful pictures of the royal baby had its inevitable consequence. One of the duties of the royal family is to be seen. When Andrew wasn't, the rumours started that there might be something wrong with him and it wasn't long before a French newspaper ran a story claiming that the Prince was malformed.

Prince Philip was furious, the Queen upset and Buckingham Palace defeated. Then, as now, they are reluctant to give way to media pressure, but in the light of this kind of speculation it was clearly self-defeating to keep Andrew hidden any longer.

So at 16 months old he made his public debut on the palace balcony for the Birthday Parade. When the crowd spotted the baby dressed in his best embroidered romper suit bobbing up and down in his mother's arms, a huge cheer went up.

The Queen and Prince Philip at Frogmore House with their children on 21 April 1965, the monarch's 39th birthday

OPPOSITE PAGE: Twelve-week-old Edward appears in public for the first time after Trooping the Colour on 13 June 1964

This was what the public wanted to see and they were reassured to learn that, far from having anything wrong with him, Andrew was the picture of health. He was heavier than Charles at that age and had the endearing habit of smiling at everyone he saw. When Sister Rowe gave her six-month progress report she called him 'a baby full of smiles'. 'He's simply wonderful in every respect,' she cooed.

Charles and Anne agreed. They were delighted with their baby brother. He seldom cried and quickly established himself as something of a character. His arrival offset the loneliness Anne had felt when Charles was sent to Cheam, and at ten she was old enough to enjoy playing mother and helping with the baby. His arrival brightened the atmosphere in the nursery suite where they all slept. In fact his arrival brightened the atmosphere throughout the palace and gave Mabel, who had taken over from Helen Lightbody, who had just left royal service, the fresh interest of a new charge to look after.

Mabel's routine varied little in the 27 years she worked at Buckingham Palace. Her father, a Liverpudlian policeman, had been killed in an air raid during the Second World War, leaving her and her Scottish mother looking for employment. Mabel, who was not a trained nursery nurse, gained her experience from working with several Scottish families before coming south. When the family she worked for moved to South America at the end of the war, they wanted Mabel to go with them but the idea did not appeal to the tall Scottish lass.

Instead she advertised her services in the 'Situations Wanted' section of a nursing magazine. The advertisement was spotted by royal nanny Helen Lightbody, who, on the instructions of her employer, was looking for an assistant. So at the age of 24, and with no formal training, Mabel Anderson found herself working for Princess Elizabeth.

Until 1980, the nursery was on the second floor above the Privy Purse entrance. Its long windows looking out over the forecourt provided an excellent vantage point for watching the sentries and the Changing of the Guard. An old-fashioned lift serviced the suite of nursery rooms, which proved useful when nanny's legs got tired and Andrew got too heavy to be carried to the Queen's private rooms on the principal floor below.

The main sitting room or playroom was large and high-ceilinged with pale green walls and an open fireplace. There was a fire and a brass fireguard on which the children's clothes were dried. A chintz-covered sofa dominated one part of the room; scaled-down chairs and tables including a miniature high-backed chair occupied another. On both sides of the fire were glass-fronted cupboards filled with toys and books from Charles and Anne's childhood. The rocking horse in the corner had belonged to the Queen, as had some of the toys, including the silver rattle Andrew liked to throw out of his pram.

Off the nursery to one side was a bathroom with a large enamel bath fitted with old-fashioned chrome taps. To the other side were the bedrooms. When Princess Anne was born, a nursery kitchen was installed; until then meals had to be brought up from the kitchens and left on a hotplate.

Mabel, who was 34 when Prince Andrew was born, ran the nursery in the traditional royal manner: unchallenged, unopposed, almost as a private fiefdom. She had the assistance of a nursery footman and an under-nanny, June Waller, who helped her in much the way she

LEFT: Edward, always more gentle than his elder brother, and Andrew with their mother at Windsor Castle in early 1965

OPPOSITE PAGE: The brothers have great fun playing in the leaves in the garden at Buckingham Palace

had helped Helen Lightbody with Charles and Anne. Royal nannies do not have to clean, cook or do the laundry. Their job is purely to see to the children's wellbeing, though Mabel did insist on Andrew's delicate baby clothes being washed by hand and dried in front of the fire as they always had been. She also insisted on the toys being tidily stacked away after use.

It was an unswerving routine, with Mabel as the pivot, and Philip and the Queen, for all her good intentions, rather remote figures.

Child psychologists argue that the love children receive in their infancy is important in the development of their ability to form adult relationships. A child that is not cuddled a great deal as a baby, they maintain, is unlikely to show affection easily, whereas one given a lot of love will probably develop into a more tactile and emotionally expressive adult.

Given the long absences of their parents, it was from the nannies that the Queen's children learned how to relate to other people and, as kind and caring as they were, it was affection that could only be given according to strict routine. That continuity gave them stability and confidence, but it did little to prepare them for the harsher realities of the outside world.

The day started at 8.15am when the children would troop in, kiss their nanny and then help themselves to a breakfast of kedgeree, scrambled eggs, tomatoes and bacon laid out on the hotplate, with either coffee or tea served in white china bearing the gold E II R cypher.

Even after she was married Anne never missed the nursery breakfast if she was staying at Buckingham Palace, and if Mark Phillips was in town he would come too.

Mabel's Roberts wireless would be tuned to BBC Radio 2, the newspapers were read, and once the plates had been cleared, Nanny would settle down to do the *Daily Telegraph* crossword. If the Queen chanced to look in, they would study the clues and Nanny would usually discover that she had gone completely wrong.

At 9.30am sharp Mabel would take the lift to the Queen and Prince Philip's private apartments on the principal floor. She would leave the baby there. But not for long. After half an hour she would return to take him back upstairs. Affairs of state could not be delayed, and when at Buckingham Palace the Queen had appointments every 20 minutes throughout the morning.

Mabel Anderson and her young charges arrive at King's Cross station, London, from Aberdeen on 8 October 1966

OPPOSITE PAGE:
The boys at King's Cross again, one year later

When Charles and Anne were younger the Queen seldom had the time to see them during the day. She would sometimes pop into the Ballroom when they had their weekly dancing lessons with Madame Vacani, but that was all. With Andrew it was slightly more relaxed, in his infancy at least, and on the occasional morning she would say, 'Leave him with me, Mabel.' Andrew would play on the floor of her study while she worked at her desk.

That was before he could walk. When he grew older he was too impish to be left to his own devices and was banished to the nursery floor. He continually tried to invade her sitting room, however, often with success, slipping past the duty page. On one occasion the page running after him failed to notice a ball Andrew had been playing with, put his foot on top of it and skidded to a halt just in front of the Queen. Hiding her amusement, she told Andrew off and sent him to put his toys away.

If the time Andrew spent with his mother was short, it was still long enough for him to observe and practise the royal wave, which he did from an early age much to the amusement of the staff, who nicknamed him Andy Pandy after the popular children's television programme of the time.

Imitation and identification are important in a child's development and Andrew soon learned that waving brought the rewarding response of people waving back and smiling. As Charles observed, the world was 'a wonderful place because everyone was always smiling'.

It was soon to be the royal wave goodbye, however, for a month before Andrew's first birthday the Queen and the Duke of Edinburgh left for a seven-week tour of India, Pakistan and Nepal.

During the tour Prince Philip, President of the World Wildlife Fund, shot a tiger and was duly mauled in the media. Back home, Andrew celebrated his first birthday with a few wobbly steps under the watchful eye of 'Gan-Gan', the Queen Mother, who enjoyed her role. 'Half the fun of being a grandmother,' she said, 'is being able to spoil your grandchildren.'

Perhaps because he was older, perhaps because he had finally found a niche for himself, Philip found fatherhood the third time around more enjoyable. He liked doing things with Andrew, took no exception when his son put his sticky fingers down his dress shirt just before he went out to dinner, and was far more patient with him than he had been with Charles or even Anne.

His appearance in the nursery filled Mabel with apprehension, however, as it had Nanny Lightbody before her. It was usually a prelude to tears, as Andrew often became over-excited when playing with his father, who had a habit of rushing away quickly to an appointment, leaving Nanny to sort out the tears – though not before once collecting a black eye in the rough and tumble.

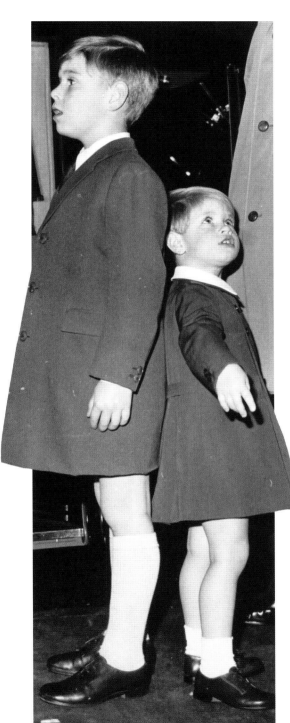

Conventional discipline did not work with Andrew, so Mabel simply dried his tears and calmed him down with a story. He adored 'Mamba', as he called her, but took a sly delight in playing her up.

The Queen communicated with her staff by memos and as soon as Andrew was old enough to realise the chaos he could cause by hiding them, he did precisely that. Even Mabel wasn't exempt from his mischief-making. On one occasion the Queen sent her page running up to the nursery demanding to know where Andrew was, which was when Mabel discovered her 'darling' had moved the memo requesting her to bring him downstairs to meet luncheon guests. She was not pleased.

When Andrew deserved it he was spanked or slapped, but in his boisterous way he soon forgot about it. The one thing that made his parents and nanny extremely angry, though, was when he was rude to others; as he was the little Prince the others were not in a position to answer back. Then the slaps really did hurt.

Once Andrew started to talk there was no stopping him, and when he was two and a half the Queen was already giving him simple lessons. She had a small blackboard, which included a clock-face and a counting frame, installed in her dining room, and after breakfast, when Mabel brought him down from the nursery, would assume the role of teacher, telling him the time and encouraging him to learn his ABC.

It was in the days before DVDs and morning television, and children's entertainment was comparatively limited. Andrew responded well for the first few minutes, but after that his concentration would wander, usually to the corgis at his mother's feet, which he would sometimes try to kick.

'A pliant and intelligent youngster with a happy disposition and full of quicksilver activity,' was how photographer Lisa Sheridan described him when she visited the palace for a session with the young Prince. He was certainly full of quicksilver activity as he kicked a football or pedalled furiously up and down the long red-carpeted corridors on his bicycle. Royal children had the use of a huge amount of space and on rainy days the corridors were where they would play cricket, hide-and-seek or football.

'I always played in the top passageway where we live,' Andrew remembered. 'We used to play football along the passageway and every now and then a pane of glass got broken, but I don't think we ever broke a piece of Meissen or anything like that!'

Like his sister, the Prince was prone to toddler tantrums and would lie on the floor screaming with rage. He was not popular with the staff, who regarded him as an unholy nuisance and felt that 'Mamba' was unable to control him when he was in one of his mischievous moods. He tormented everyone, from the nursery corgis to the scarlet-coated sentries in their tall bearskins with bayonets fixed to their rifles. He too used to walk up and down in front of them, forcing them to present arms as protocol demanded.

From a very early age Andrew had what came to be seen as an arrogant disregard for the palace staff. He would treat them like servants, and no effort by Mabel could modify his attitude. He used to thump the footman from behind with a clenched fist, then run along the corridor shouting 'Get me! Get me!'

Mabel, in exasperation, would give his chubby bottom a slap. It made no difference. Andrew took a little more notice of his mother, who would slap him around the back of the legs, reducing him to tears and the yells of hurt pride.

The Queen, Prince Philip and their offspring in the grounds of Frogmore House, 21 April 1968

OPPOSITE PAGE: In a scene from Her Majesty's 1971 Christmas broadcast, Andrew and Edward look through a family photograph album

In a behavioural study of New York toddlers, 95 per cent had 'stubborn attention-seeking behaviour'. Andrew was just naughtier than most, a genetic inheritance from his father: Andrew was a chip off the old block. He even looked like Philip as a child. Princess Alice, Philip's eccentric deaf mother, who by the time Andrew was born was living at Buckingham Palace, thought Andrew was just like her only son.

She noticed him hunching his shoulders about his ears when anything excited or amused him, just as Philip had done.

Sculptor Franta Belsky disagreed. She was commissioned by the Queen Mother to fashion a bronze of the then three-year-old Andrew before he lost his baby looks, and studied him with an artist's eye over eight sittings. He had the Queen Mother's brow, the Windsor mouth and nose, but his father's colouring and shape of head, she concluded. Franta kept Andrew amused with picture books, toys and chocolate money during the sittings, but by far the most successful ploy was to give him some clay of his own to mould into shapes.

'I have never seen such sustained concentration and excitement of discovery in a child,' she said later.

This early concentration didn't always follow Andrew into the schoolroom; only if something really interested him would he give his full attention.

As she had done with Anne, the Queen arranged for children of a similar age to join Andrew for his lessons with Miss Peebles. There were two boys, Justin Beaumont and James Steel, and two girls, Katie Seymour and Victoria Buder, the daughter of Lord Dunboyne.

The arrival of Edward on 10 March 1964 was a surprise to Andrew, who had been told he was getting a playmate, not a little baby who looked like a doll. It was a surprise to everyone else for other reasons. The Queen was not expecting the baby for another week and was startled when her contractions began earlier than anticipated.

At 8.20pm the Queen gave birth to a 5lb 7oz baby boy in the Belgian Suite, where once again the large bathroom had been converted into a delivery room. The medical team, again headed by her surgeon-gynaecologist John Peel, had thought the baby would be a girl because of its size. The Queen thought so too.

Indeed, so convinced was she that she had only discussed girls' names with her husband, and it was not for several days after the birth that the infant Prince's names were finalised.

On 2 May the six-week-old Prince was christened Edward Antony Richard Louis in the private chapel at Windsor Castle. Because of the confusion over the baby's sex and subsequent disagreements over his name, the Queen and Philip decided to choose the godparents first and use them as the child's middle names: Antony after Antony Armstrong-Jones; Richard after the present Duke of Gloucester and Louis after Prince Louis of Hesse. The godmothers were Prince Philip's sister Sophie and the Duchess of Kent, who had just given birth to a baby girl herself and was unable to attend the christening. Her mother-in-law, Princess Marina, stood proxy for her.

The birth of Edward did little to alter the unswerving routine of the nursery. While Mabel Anderson looked after the baby with the help of a maternity nurse, Andrew and his friends carried on with their lessons in the schoolroom. Every morning at 11 o'clock everything stopped and Miss Peebles, Mabel, the nurse and other nursery staff would have a cup of tea together.

The children were allowed orange juice or Ribena – Andrew once spilt his glass of the blackcurrant drink over the Queen Mother – and a biscuit. If they had been good, they were allowed just one boiled sweet before starting work again. Andrew always rummaged for a black one (as his daughter

Much amusement in the car as the royal family are driven from Crathie Kirk during their annual holiday on Deeside

OPPOSITE PAGE: The Princes, their mother and cousin Sarah Armstrong-Jones set off for Sandringham on 29 December 1971

Eugenie would do 30 years later). The Queen didn't eat many sweets or approve of her children doing so, but if they were going on a long journey, Nanny would always carry a bag of boiled sweets and Kit-Kat chocolate bars.

It was as normal an existence as the Queen could hope for, but by any standards it was extremely protected. The only children Andrew mixed with apart from his family were his little school friends. Attempts were made for him to integrate with children from less well-to-do backgrounds, but they failed. He joined the local Cub pack, but because of worries about security it was deemed wiser if the Cubs came to him, so once a week a minibus carrying the other Cubs arrived for a meeting at Buckingham Palace. Andrew was indifferent. He enjoyed their company, but because the meetings were held in his back garden, it simply didn't provide the excitement felt by the other boys.

It was the same when he went to a private gymnasium for lessons in physical training. It was the same when he was taken secretly to the Brigade of Guards' sports ground to learn to kick a football or was given tuition by former Wimbledon tennis champion Dan Maskell.

It was the same when Andrew went skating and was tutored by the resident professional, Ron Lee. When the little Prince appeared, the other skaters were ordered off the rink. And later, when he wanted to learn cricket and was taken to Lord's cricket ground at St John's Wood, he was taught by professional cricketer Len Muncer.

It was a young life filled with special privilege. His mother's desire for him to lead a normal existence was becoming less and less likely to be fulfilled. However, his lively personality obliterated all traces of shyness when dealing with strangers, as Cecil Beaton observed when he went back to Buckingham Palace on 22 May 1964.

'The children with their nonchalant nannies and nurses give the Palace a sense of reality that necessarily it lacks. I asked Andrew if he minded my taking photographs of him tomorrow. He smiled and said, "No, I don't mind". A welcome contrast to a reply I might have got from Princess Anne.'

The following day Beaton returned for the session itself. 'I waited in the Picture Gallery looking at some of the rather boring pictures, including a dull Vermeer. 'There he is,' said the Queen in a loud little girl's voice, and Andrew ran towards me, cheerful, polite and willing to please. At the end of the gallery... was the Queen accompanied by her newborn in the arms of a nurse. My heart lifted as I noticed the Queen was wearing rather a beautiful colour – a Thai silk dress – almost as light in tone as I would have wished...

'The mouth when smiling is delightfully generous. The infant showed bonhomie and an interest in the activity that was going on. His adult behaviour pleased the Queen, who was in a happy and contented and calm mood – and not only smiled at my instructions but with amusement at the activities and fast developing character of the newborn. Andrew was determined to be in every picture and behaved like a professional, adding the quality of charm of the too young to know what it is all about.

With Charles and Anne away at boarding school, Andrew and Edward should have been able to enjoy the undivided attention of their parents, but the reins of the monarchy were always pulling.

Even during the weekends at Windsor she was busy with affairs of state and surrounded by members of the Royal Household.

When the Queen and Prince Philip did join their children, it was for tea in the nursery. They never arrived unannounced and the staff always knew when one of them was coming. Mabel would fuss around making sure everything was in place and the children were clean and tidy. Sometimes on Mabel's day off or when she went to her evening pottery classes, the Queen would babysit with the two children.

It was still very formal, however, and she would bring her own page and footman, who would serve her supper in front of the nursery television. If the children awoke she would soothe them back to sleep. She relished those rare private moments with her children, and in later years admitted that she felt guilty about not spending more time with them.

There was no escape from the merry-go-round of royal engagements, but the Queen and Philip would never go out to dinner without saying goodnight to their children. If they were going out to an official function such as a film premiere, Mispy or Nanny would take them out into the corridor so they could wave goodbye. Before she got into the car wearing her tiara and long dress the Queen would always look up to the nursery floor and, seeing their anxious little faces pressed against the glass, give them a wave. Philip would blow a kiss. Always.

Charles also took an interest. When Philip was away and the Queen otherwise engaged, he would make a point of going into the nursery to play with his brothers and read them

stories. One summer while they were cruising around the Western Isles of Scotland aboard HMY *Britannia*, he wrote a story for nine-year-old Andrew and five-year-old Edward and called it *The Old Man of Lochnagar*.

The Queen and Philip's theories about bringing up children had been tempered by experience. As Philip explained: 'It's no good saying, do this, do that, don't do this, don't do that,' he has said. 'It's very easy when children want to do something to say no immediately. I think it's quite important not to give an unequivocal answer at once. Much better to think it over. Then, if you eventually say no, I think they really accept it.'

Perhaps there weren't enough 'no's' in Andrew's young life. He bullied everybody and would constantly swipe his younger brother. If he saw Edward going for a particular cake, Andrew would try to grab it first. He tried to provoke him, but Edward wasn't going to be provoked.

When the Queen wasn't around, Philip took charge of the children, but he became easily distracted and often let them wander off. One weekend when he was five, Andrew made his way to the Royal Mews at Windsor while his father was out carriage-driving. The coachmen and grooms who worked there had little time for the Prince, whom they had seen taunting the dogs and aiming sly kicks at helpless Guardsmen. Sensing their studied indifference and in order to attract attention, the Prince started beating the ground with a large stick.

No one took any notice, so Andrew doubled his efforts and beat the ground even harder, taking a sideways swipe at the legs of the horses. When he refused to stop, two grooms picked him up, threw him into a dung heap and shovelled manure all over him.

The Prince was too shocked to cry. But the impact of his humiliation hit him, and when at last he managed to extricate himself from the foul-smelling mess, he ran as fast as his legs could carry him up the hill to the castle shouting, 'I'll tell my Mummy! I'll tell my Mummy on you!' No one knows if he ever did, but there were no repercussions.

Nor were there on another occasion when his taunting so annoyed a young footman that he took a swipe at Andrew that deposited him on the floor and left him with a glistening black eye. Fearing for his job, the footman confessed what had

LEFT: On his eighth birthday Edward leaves Gibbs school in Kensington for Buckingham Palace, where a party and film show were to take place

OPPOSITE PAGE: The Queen, in mourning for her uncle, the Duke of Windsor, talks to her youngest son in the palace quadrangle in June 1972

happened and offered his resignation. When the Queen came to hear of it she refused to accept it. She said her son had obviously deserved it and that the footman was on no account to be punished for Andrew's bad behaviour.

Edward by contrast was the 'quiet one'. He was a 'sweet' child, whose delicate good looks and permanently flushed cheeks endeared him to the staff. While Andrew was almost permanently bored as an adolescent at Buckingham Palace, Edward enjoyed the solitude and spent his time reading and listening to the radio. They all loved the radio and always listened to Radio 2 until Terry Wogan went off the air. Then Edward moved to Capital Radio, Anne to Radio 1 and Charles to Radio 4. Andrew preferred cassette tapes. Edward enjoyed the radio so much he had a special wooden case made so that he could take his Roberts everywhere with him. If mislaid, footmen were sent scurrying to look for it.

As a child he loved books and as soon as he learnt to read he devoured everything, from the popular classics to detective thrillers. He also liked the French cartoon books, *Asterix*, which he would read in French. 'He was extremely bright,' a member of staff remembers. The Swedish pop group Abba were his favourite listening. But the Prince's great enjoyment was riding and as soon as he was old enough to sit on a pony, riding lessons became the high point of his day.

Edward became an accomplished horseman. His first pony was a Shetland pony named Valkyrie that he shared with his older brother. But whereas Andrew liked grooming the pony and putting on its tack, Edward liked sitting on its back.

It sounded a perfect solution, but as soon as Andrew realised his little brother was going to ride the pony away he would try and lead Valkyrie back to her stable to take her harness off.

Between the ages of four and eight Andrew had been educated in the security of the Buckingham Palace schoolroom by Miss Peebles, and it was assumed that Edward would follow in his educational footsteps. But just before he was due to start his formal education in September 1968, 'dear Miss P' was found dead in her room. She had ruled the schoolroom for 15 years. Suddenly a replacement had to be found.

The Queen's lady-in-waiting, Lady Susan Hussey, sportingly offered her own governess, Miss Adele Grigg, who ran a class from her Chelsea home. She taught Edward for two months until a new governess, Miss Lavinia Keppel, was engaged.

Miss Keppel was a relation of the famous Alice Keppel, for many years the mistress of Edward VII – intriguing proof that there are different ways to serve the royal family. She had first taught at Lady Eden's school in Kensington and had a more modern outlook on education, but still followed Miss P's basic pattern of lessons. The day always began with prayers and a Bible story and included some kind of physical activity.

Still pursuing the grail of integration, the Queen was keen that Edward mix with other children, and the schoolroom always had at least three other little pupils in it.

Lady Sarah Armstrong-Jones, James Ogilvy and Princess Tania of Hanover, a granddaughter of Philip's sister Sophie, were regulars and the children of members of the Royal Household sometimes joined them. It proved a successful experiment for both Andrew and Edward.

Anne and Charles had dreaded their first day at boarding school. She had been physically sick and Charles so frightened that he shook. This was not the case with Andrew, who at the age of eight and a half was sent to Heatherdown, near Ascot, conveniently close to Windsor Castle, or indeed with Edward, who followed him there two years later after a spell at Gibbs pre-preparatory school in Kensington.

In the holidays Mabel transported the familiar atmosphere of the nursery to wherever they were. At Balmoral, the nursery quarters were in a corner turret. Prince Edward had a tiny bedroom next to Mabel's, but the routine was unchanged. Lunch was always a picnic and the children had supper in their dressing gowns after a bath.

'Sixteen was the golden age of going downstairs,' a member of staff recalls, 'but they preferred to be in the nursery after a day outside far more than being downstairs with the guests.'

At half term, Edward would often spend time at Wood Farm on the Sandringham estate with only his nanny and a nursery footman for company. Housekeeper Mrs Hazel cleaned and cooked simple fare – corn on the cob perhaps or the fishcakes that Edward loved – and the Prince went for long walks on the beach. At Windsor, all Edward wanted to do was ride his pony, Flame, and would be quite happy when left alone to do so. If he was thwarted in any way his bad temper manifested itself in silence. If he were very angry he would go bright red but he never shouted or screamed, unlike Andrew.

Nearly a decade and a sizeable spiritual and emotional gap separated Andrew and Edward from Charles and Anne; although subjected to the same kind of upbringing and accorded the same kind of privileges, the atmosphere was more relaxed and they were better equipped to deal with public-school life, where the regimented routine was not so different from their own. By the time they both started school, the Swinging Sixties had come and gone, and unemployment and Northern Ireland were the kingdom's main preoccupations.

While unemployment was not a problem they had to deal with, the deteriorating situation in Northern Ireland meant an inevitable increase in royal security and when, during the Christmas holidays of 1970, Special Branch learned of an IRA plot to kidnap either Andrew or his cousin George, Earl of St Andrews, who was also at Heatherdown, the guard was increased.

These royal protection officers (armed bodyguards would be a more accurate description) do their best to merge into the background, though some inevitably become great friends of their 'clients'. Andrew Merrylees, who was appointed a bodyguard to the Prince when he was nine years old, remained with him throughout his schooldays and left 18 years later. 'Edward looked upon him as a substitute father, as his own was often away,' a member of staff once confided.

Although Philip was affectionate with them when he was around, he did not agree with indulging children. They were given pocket money but only used it to buy records and tapes. They didn't have many clothes and never bought their own. Edward wore Andrew's hand-me-downs.

When it came to senior schooling, Eton was once again considered, as it had been with Charles, but again Prince Philip could not be convinced. He remained a sternly devout disciple of Kurt Hahn's guiding principle: character first, intelligence second, knowledge third. Gordonstoun in faraway Morayshire, he insisted, would be far better for them.

For Andrew, who was not intellectual, perhaps it was. He was not timid like his elder brother and soon acquired a not-so-enviable reputation as a joke-teller.

ABOVE: Prince Edward cuddles a black Labrador pup during a visit to the kennels at Balmoral in September 1972

OPPOSITE PAGE: Two months later, on 20 November, he and his siblings were celebrating the Queen and Prince Philip's Silver Wedding anniversary

'Andrew never stopped cracking jokes,' one of his former classmates recalled. 'Goodness knows where he got them from, but whatever the source, it showed no signs of drying up.'

Another Gordonstoun schoolmate said that he became known as the 'Sniggerer' because of his tendency to sidle up to someone and say, 'Have you heard the one about...'

'The trouble is, by the time he had finished the joke he was laughing so much you couldn't understand the punch line.'

One girl in the same class as Prince Andrew at the by now co-educational school remembered him as 'a man with a fat bottom who laughed at his own jokes'.

Perhaps Eton would have polished Andrew's rough corners

and given him a better scholastic education. He was less adaptable than Charles, and judging by the comments made by his contemporaries, it is clear that his 'I am the Prince' attitude stood out at the determinedly egalitarian school.

One fellow pupil regarded him as just another sad little rich kid who 'didn't know whether he wanted to be a prince or one of the lads'. His inability to resolve that dilemma proved something of a handicap, and he did not emulate his father and elder brother by becoming Guardian.

Edward did. The Queen's youngest child had loathed the idea of going to Gordonstoun and in the beginning felt singled out and different, if only because of the police protectors who had become a permanent appendage to all royal personages. But once he had settled in he found that he enjoyed outdoor activities like sailing and rock-climbing, and would later speak of his time there with some enthusiasm. But the Prince never considered schooldays 'fun'.

'A school is a school,' he said later. 'I don't agree with the statement that school days are the happiest days of your life.'

Edward was a solitary person who preferred to do things his own way. Three A-levels got him into Cambridge (amidst criticism from those who said that his status had more to do with his being granted a place than his middling grades), and the relative freedom he enjoyed there gave him a taste of a world not normally accorded to royal princes. He liked that.

Neither Edward nor Andrew ever expanded to his full potential as an adult. They were quite loving children, but neither of them was generous. They both enjoyed play-acting, but not the real life their sheltered upbringing had ill prepared them for. They were also more immature than most of their contemporaries – would other children at the age of 15, for instance, still be having supper in their dressing gowns with Nanny in the nursery?

They had little say when it first came to the vital matter of choosing their careers. It had to be the military. As Andrew pointed out, what other real choice was there for a prince?

As it turned out, Andrew thoroughly enjoyed the Royal Navy. Edward's military career, on the other hand, was disastrously short-lived.

He joined the Royal Marines. In the crisis of late adolescence

LEFT: The Duke of Edinburgh and Prince Andrew on board the ocean yacht *Yeoman XIX* at Cowes during the 1973 regatta

OPPOSITE PAGE: The Queen and Prince Edward shield their ears at RAF Finningley whilst attending the Silver Jubilee review of the Royal Air Force in July 1977

he left before his training had been completed. His parents pleaded with him to reconsider and stay after completing a year. Edward, as he always has done when faced with something unpleasant, switched off before allowing his emotions to escape in the privacy of his room, where he wept.

After more discussions with his parents at Sandringham and with his commandant, Sir Michael Watkins, the pressure was so great he agreed – for his sister's sake – to a meeting, without his parents, at Buckingham Palace.

Anne, Mark Phillips, Fergie and Andrew drove to London on Sunday 11 January 1987 to meet Edward. They spent the afternoon talking to him gently, explaining to him that it made

sense to stay in the Marines for another eight months, and then announce he had decided not to pursue any more training. Without the presence of the Queen and Philip the situation seemed less oppressive and eventually Edward agreed.

Anne, immensely relieved that her brother had saved himself so much anguish, returned that night to Gatcombe Park with her husband. The following morning, as she was driving to Sandringham in her Range Rover, she heard on the radio news that Edward had quit. So great was her shock that she almost drove the car into a ditch. 'My God!' she exclaimed. 'He's going to regret that for the rest of his life!'

It was Edward's first adult decision in the real world.

The Hon. Diana Spencer at Park House, Sandringham, Norfolk, on her first birthday, 1 July 1962

Diana

SIXTEEN DAYS BEFORE Christmas 1968, Viscountess Althorp started proceedings in the High Court in London to end her 14-year marriage to the 7th Earl Spencer's son and heir, Johnny. She was 32, her husband 44. Diana, their youngest daughter, was only seven.

The divorce quickly degenerated into a painful contest that pitted husband against wife, turned Lady Althorp's mother, Ruth, Lady Fermoy, against her daughter, and eventually lost Lady Althorp the custody of her four children. It left their youngest daughter with a psychological injury from which she struggled to recover.

Diana remembered the arguments that led to the separation. She could still hear the sound of her mother crying and the resonance of her father's harsh words that had provoked those tears. There were occasions when his temper drove him to violence. Too young to intervene, too immature to cope, she took the only course open to her and locked her feelings away inside herself.

Some children come to terms with such early traumas: to confront them, to move on, eventually to accept them as a sad but unalterable chapter of their lives. As Erin Pizzey, Britain's foremost counsellor of abused women and their children, explained: 'We all have to come to terms with our childhoods in order to cope with adult life.'

Diana never did. The emotional lesion was allowed to fester untreated and would later manifest itself in an eating disorder, bulimia. Sufferers, convinced of their own worthlessness and frightened of failure, binge-eat before making themselves sick.

'Most bulimics have a history of early emotional starvation and it must be remembered that Diana's mother left her when she was very young,' psychotherapist Patricia Peters wrote in *The Sunday Times*. 'Self-esteem is shattered when a mother leaves her child. The concept is, "My mother couldn't have

loved me or she wouldn't have left me", and the depression that follows is an expression of the anger which is turned against the self.'

In fact, Diana's mother did not want to leave her children. She battled in the courts for four months to keep custody of Diana and her other children, Sarah, Jane and their little brother, Charles.

It was Frances Althorp herself who initiated the action to end her marriage. Filing for divorce at that time demanded very specific circumstances: under the Marital Causes Act 1965 a divorce could be sought only on the grounds of adultery, desertion 'without cause' for a period of three years, a clause that included insanity, or 'on the grounds that her husband has since the celebration of the marriage been guilty of rape, sodomy or bestiality…'

None of those applied, but there was one more category – 'cruelty'. The destructive confrontations of the kind that the infant Diana had witnessed 'from her hiding place behind the drawing-room door' gave Frances the grounds on which to seek to end her marriage. As one who knew the couple put it starkly: 'Johnny Althorp could be horrid.'

Frances was herself an adulteress who had been named as the 'other woman' in an uncontested suit brought against her lover, Peter Shand Kydd, by his wife, Elizabeth. In the late Sixties, before the law adapted to the radical change in social attitudes that took place during that decade, that still weighed heavily against a woman. Viscount Althorp cross-petitioned and won. The divorce was granted in April 1969 by Mr Justice Wrangham on the grounds of Lady Althorp's adultery.

The judge awarded Althorp custody of the children and ordered Diana's mother and Shand Kydd to pay £3,000 legal costs. It was a social and maternal humiliation for Frances. It would have a dire effect on their children.

For a long time after the final split Diana's brother, Charles, would cry himself to sleep at night, calling out for a mother no longer there. Sarah, Diana's eldest sister, would later develop anorexia nervosa, a disease closely related to bulimia. Erin Pizzey, who founded Chiswick Women's Aid in 1971 to help battered women and their children, said: 'Diana forcibly lost her mother when she was very young and this loss – of a good, warm, loving figure – would have had a major effect on her.

'If you don't resolve the damage you take it with you into adulthood where it can affect your relationships with men. She would have grown up with a great deal of fear and probably have over-compensated with her own children. She would be anxious to give back what she had lost.'

There was little their father could do to reduce this long-term damage. He was a man who always did his civic duty, but he believed that it was a woman's job to look after the children and had not the faintest idea how to tend to the needs of his distraught brood. He also happened to be suffering from what his son later described as 'shell shock'.

Looking back at the ruin of his marriage, Johnny asked: 'How many of those 14 years were happy? I thought all of them, until the moment we parted. I was wrong.'

Frances and Johnny became engaged in October 1953. She had known him, it was reported at the time, 'since she was a schoolgirl'. That was no time at all. Frances was 17 years old when she became betrothed.

The period of their engagement did not allow them an opportunity to get to know each other any better; three weeks after their engagement was announced, Johnny left for the Queen's six-month post-coronation tour of the Commonwealth. He took with him a portrait of his fiancée painted in red oxide by the society artist Nicholas Egon, which he hung in his cabin aboard *Gothic*, the royal tour liner.

Viscount Althorp and his bride, the former Frances Roche, at Westminster Abbey after their wedding in June 1954

OPPOSITE PAGE: Diana in the stately family pram in 1963

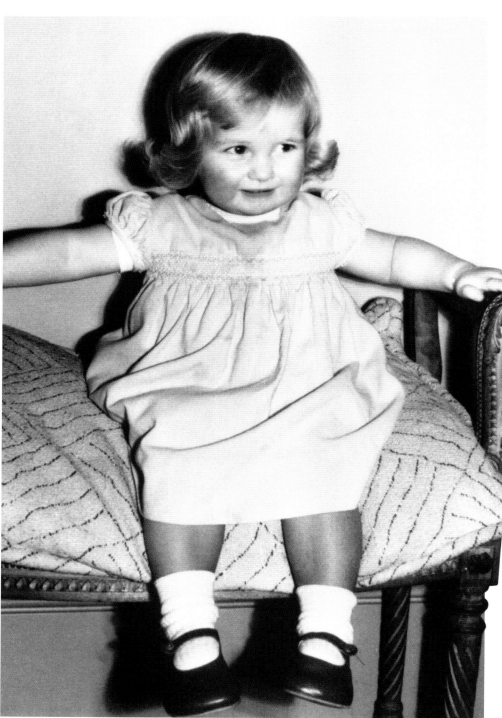

Frances was still only 18 when she married the 30-year-old heir to the Spencer earldom in a lavish ceremony at Westminster Abbey the following June. She was the youngest bride to be married there in over half a century.

The service was attended by 1,500 guests including the Queen, the Duke of Edinburgh, the Queen Mother, Princess Margaret (in the middle of the 'Townsend affair'), the Princess Royal, Countess of Harewood, the duchesses of Kent and Gloucester, the young Duke of Kent and his sister, Princess Alexandra.

The bride wore a gown of 'camellia-coloured faille embroidered on the tight-fitting bodice and full skirt with hand-cut diamonds, sequins and rhinestones, and a tulle veil which formed a short train and was held in place by a diamond tiara'.

The service was followed by a lavish reception for 800 – all nine members of the royal family attended – at St James's Palace, which the Queen had lent for the occasion. It was a splash of high life to brighten the austere, glamour-starved Britain of the Fifties and was declared 'the wedding of the year'.

Sarah was born the following year, Jane two years later. The Spencers made their home at Park House, a ten-room Victorian mansion on the royal Sandringham estate in Norfolk that Frances's father, who died in 1955, had leased from his friend, King George VI.

Having left royal service, Johnny studied at the Royal Agricultural College, Cirencester, and started to farm the 650 nearby acres bought in part with £20,000 of his young wife's inheritance.

To all outward appearances they were a contented, well-to-do country family, rooted to the land, filling in their time with good works and civic duties. The seeds of their future troubles had already been planted, however, though Johnny, so decent, and essentially so naive, didn't realise it.

He had served with the Royal Scots Greys in the war (and been mentioned in dispatches) and then as aide-de-camp to the governor of South Australia. He had seen the world and now wanted to enjoy the life of a country squire before he inherited his father's title and responsibilities.

The same was not true of his wife. She was young and had never had the opportunity of enjoying her youth. She was married to a man 12 years older than herself and soon became bored with the deadening routine of her life.

In 1960 she gave birth to her third child, a son named John, who died ten hours later. Johnny felt it his duty to produce an heir: they tried again and on 1 July 1961 Frances gave birth to another child. It was not, however, the son Johnny had so set his heart on that he had considered only boys' names. It was another girl.

A week later she was named Diana Frances and declared a 'perfect physical specimen' by her father. The need to produce a son to inherit the earldom remained of paramount importance to Johnny. He blamed Frances for the failure (despite it being the male contribution to the pregnancy which actually determines the sex of the child). She was sent to Harley Street for tests.

'It was a dreadful time for my parents and probably the root of their divorce because I don't think they ever got over it,' Charles, the son who did eventually arrive, would much later say.

Diana formed her own poignant opinion on the subject: 'I was supposed to be a boy.' To add to her sense of inferiority, to the feeling that she was in some way a 'nuisance' to her parents, Diana came to believe that, had that first boy survived, she would not have been born at all.

That might have been true, but if her parents lacked insight into the emotional needs of their daughter, Diana's childhood nevertheless had its compensations.

RIGHT: Diana showed an early interest in clothes and loved the red jacket and matching shoes in which she is pictured

OPPOSITE PAGE: The future Princess, pretty as a picture as a two-year-old at Park House

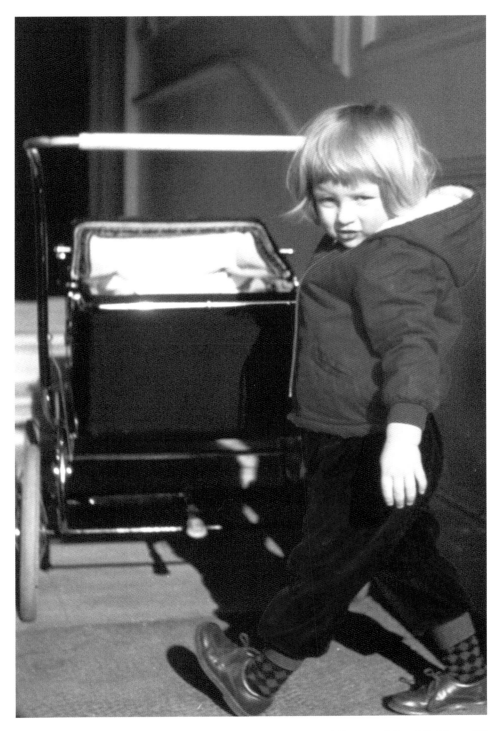

Park House was the ideal setting for young children: big, rambling and very homely. There were romps with her father in the nursery, 'a wonderful room for playing bears in', as he recalled. Diana was surrounded by animals – rabbits, hamsters and gerbils, gun dogs, a springer spaniel named Jill, and Marmalade the cat. There were woods and fields to roam in, and country lanes to ride her bicycle along.

There were ponies and horses, though Diana did not care for them. She had taken up riding at the age of three but when she was eight had fallen off and broken her arm. She fell off again two years later when her pony caught its foot in a rabbit hole. 'We walked the rest of the way home and the doctor checked her out and said she was fine,' Mary Clarke, her nanny at the time, recalled. Fear got the better of her and it was not until she married that she mounted a horse again.

Diana much preferred the outdoor heated swimming pool where she developed her diving technique, and the family's summer visits to the seaside at Brancaster to bathe and build sandcastles on the beach. There were also visits to the 'big house' for tea with Prince Andrew and later Prince Edward, who succeeded in covering himself with honey.

'The children were socialising all the time and Diana loved parties,' recalled Janet Thompson, her nanny for two and a half years.

Diana saw little of her parents, it is true, as she spent most of her time in the company of her nannies and her governess, Gertrude Allen, who had once taught her mother. But that was not unusual, given the Althorps' social background, and she was certainly never left to fend for herself.

'The Althorp children never tidied their rooms or made their beds,' Nanny Thompson said. There was no need to. The Althorps employed six members of staff, including a full-time cook. We're not at all grand,' Frances would say. That depends on your definition of grand; Mary Clarke felt that she was 'seeing a bit of old England that was dying fast'.

Charles Althorp, who was born three years after Diana, agreed. 'It was a privileged upbringing out of a different age.' Not that they regarded it as such. 'As children we accepted our circumstances as normal,' he said. But for all the comfort and advantages something, as Charles said, was certainly lacking: 'a mother figure'.

In the summer of 1966 Frances met Edinburgh University-educated wallpaper heir Peter Shand Kydd at a dinner party in London. He was everything her husband was not – witty, raffish, extrovert and blessed with an ability to make women laugh. They soon became lovers. Within a few indecent months Shand Kydd had left his wife and three children and Frances had moved out of Park House with her children and into an apartment in Cadogan Place in Chelsea to be near him.

Sometimes Johnny would come to London to visit them at weekends and holidays. But it was an unsatisfactory state of affairs and, badly wounded by his wife's defection, he made up his mind that he, not their mother, would have care and control of all the children.

Johnny Althorp doted on his youngest daughter but it was his son, who would one day inherit his title and his lands, who was the object of his familial ambition – a point made very clear by the religious ceremonies held to mark their respective births.

Diana was christened at St Mary Magdalene, the local church in Sandringham. Her godparents were John Floyd, Alexander Gilmour, Mrs Timothy Colman, Mrs William Fox and Mrs Michael Pratt, worthy friends of her parents.

Charles, on the other hand, was christened in Westminster Abbey with the Queen as one of his godparents. Althorp had waited ten years for his son and he had no intention of losing him.

Frances returned to Park House for the Christmas of 1967 for the sake of the children. It was the last time the family would be together.

Johnny, consumed with rage, was in a dark and violent mood. His self-control deserted him and his rows with Frances were extreme. She cried and pleaded but her husband was adamant: the children, he insisted, would stay with him.

'He refused to let them return to London,' Frances said. She, in turn, refused to stay with her husband and returned to the capital, leaving the two youngest children behind (Sarah and Jane were at boarding school).

'It had become apparent that the marriage had broken down completely,' she added.

Althorp was incapable of looking after the children by himself, and the following February he advertised for a nanny to take 'full charge' of them. So began an even more unsettled period in their young lives, with nannies coming and going with distressing regularity.

'As children we accepted this as quite normal,' Charles Althorp recalled. 'But now it seems so frightening.

'We were very lucky in that we had three or four nannies during those years who were exceptionally nice, devoted, loving people – but there were some strange ones as well.

'There was one, I believe, who attacked my father with a carving knife. She didn't catch him, then disappeared shouting, "To the river, to the river!" That was the last we saw of her!'

LEFT: Diana Spencer poses for a photograph taken by her father in London's Cadogan Place Gardens in the summer of 1968

OPPOSITE PAGE: Diana as a chubby three-year-old in the garden of her home in rural Norfolk, where she spent much of her childhood

Diana was 'seriously affected' by the breakdown of her parents' marriage, Nanny Clarke thought. Once so lively, the little girl staff nicknamed 'Duchess' became introverted and nervous and acquired the lifelong habit of looking down.

Always headstrong, she became even more wilful and on occasion downright disobedient. She resented the parade of nannies she believed were trying to usurp her mother's place.

'Manners were very important,' Nanny Clarke remembered.

In the confusion generated by Lady Althorp's departure they were often forgotten. Diana locked one nanny in a bathroom. She threw another's clothes on to the roof. Sometimes the nannies responded in kind. One used to bang Diana and Charles's heads together. There were, Diana recalled, 'too many nannies. The whole thing was very unstable'.

Her father found it hard to cope. He did not have the required skills to be a single parent. He never spoke to them about the problems that engulfed the family, Diana would later complain. He would sometimes join them for tea in the nursery but it was, so Nanny Clarke recalled, 'very hard going. In those early days after the divorce he wasn't very relaxed with them.'

Their mother, who married Shand Kydd within a month of her divorce, continued to see her children, but was not in a position to assuage their distress. Whatever the background to the divorce – Johnny was not as easy to live with as his later image of a warm-hearted, tweedy, country man, might have suggested – Frances would hereafter be labelled a 'bolter', condemned to carry the stigma of a woman who had run out on her family and her responsibilities.

Diana never publicly criticised her mother for her actions. It was notable to her friends that the adult Diana did not mention her name if she could avoid it. Her sense of rejection became embedded, and all the holidays she spent with her mother and all the presents Frances lavished on her did not alleviate it. She felt unwanted, a feeling compounded when she was sent away to boarding school shortly afterwards.

Diana had been to school before – in London, when she briefly lived there with her mother, then to Silfield, a pre-prep in King's Lynn; but that had been a day school and every afternoon she had returned home. The atmosphere at Park House may not have been a happy one – filled with her own anxieties, the silence of the country night played on her terrified imagination. She had no mother on hand to comfort her and would lie awake, listening to her brother crying in his sleep, too frightened to get out of bed to soothe him. But it was still her home, full of familiar objects and the animals she loved.

There was Charles to help dress and a teddy bear to dress in the clothes her little brother had outgrown. 'She's always had a very loving nature,' Charles Althorp said. 'She was very good with me as a baby. She used to look after me.'

Now Diana was being wrenched away from the only security she had left. Her parents had decided that it would be in their troubled daughter's best interests for her to have the routine and discipline of a traditional English boarding school. Riddlesworth Hall, 40 miles from Sandringham, was selected.

LEFT: Diana Spencer with her four-year-old brother Charles, Viscount Althorp (later 9th Earl Spencer) in 1968

OPPOSITE PAGE: In 1970 Diana went to stay with her mother and stepfather, Peter Shand Kydd, at Itchenor, West Sussex

Johnny Althorp drove her there and left her clutching a stuffed green hippopotamus and Peanuts, her pet guinea pig. It was, he recalled, 'a terrible day'. So it was for his eight-year-old daughter as well. It was the beginning of eight years of institutional care, first at Riddlesworth and later at West Heath, the smart girls' public school in Kent which her mother and sisters had attended.

As it turned out, Diana settled in quite well. The British boarding school can be an intimidating institution but by its insistence on rules and order it can provide a sense of security – exactly what Diana needed.

She made friends. She was good at sport – she was an excellent diver and did well at netball because, as she said, 'it was much easier for me to get the ball in the net because I was so tall'. She excelled at dancing. And if she could be a little boisterous on occasion — she was an enthusiastic participant in dormitory romps, midnight feasts and custard-pie fights, and if she didn't like a particular sporting activity she would smear her knees with blue eye-shadow and pretend it was bruising – that was more than compensated for by her attitude towards others.

Joan Lowe, her headmistress at Silfield, recalled her 'kindness to the smaller members of the community'. At West Heath she became involved in community work in nearby Sevenoaks, paying regular visits to old people to sit and talk with them for hours. It came naturally to her: she had an intuitive sympathy for others and enjoyed the work. She also visited Darenth Park mental hospital for the Voluntary Service Unit.

Some found the experience harrowing. Not Diana. Always most at ease with people older or less fortunate than herself, she derived satisfaction from trying to elicit a word or a smile from the physically and mentally handicapped inmates. Muriel Stevens, who helped to organise those visits, said: 'That's where she learned to go down on her hands and knees to meet people because most of the interaction was crawling with the patients.'

On the academic front, however, Diana was always in difficulties. She was, Jean Lowe recalled diplomatically, 'extremely average'.

Her brother, spotting her difficulties, unkindly nicknamed her Brian after the dim-witted snail in the children's television programme *The Magic Roundabout*. Diana learned enough at Riddlesworth to pass the Common Entrance examination that gave her her passage to West Heath, but the rigours of study all but defeated her. She took a modest five O-levels and failed every one.

Her middle sister, Jane, who was a senior girl when Diana arrived, had passed her O-levels and had gone on to take A-levels. Her elder sister Sarah's education was disrupted when she was expelled for drinking.

RIGHT: Whilst holidaying at Itchenor in 1970 barefoot Diana plays a game of croquet, despite the mallet being almost as tall as her

OPPOSITE PAGE: Diana sports a traditional tweed hat during a visit to Uist in the Western Isles, Scotland, in 1974

'I was bored,' she explained. Her brother, however, sailed through Eton and went on to Oxford University. Diana, still very unsure of herself, found the comparisons odious. She felt herself to be 'hopeless, a dropout'. Confronted with those stark academic results, Diana had no choice but to do exactly that and drop out of school, an unqualified 16-year-old without obvious prospects but with the not inconsiderable advantage of her family's name and wealth to fall back on.

In 1975 Diana's irascible grandfather died. Johnny Althorp was now the 8th Earl Spencer, owner of one of the finest houses in Britain and, despite the taxing problem of over two million pounds' death duties, a very rich man. As the daughter of an earl, she was now Lady Diana Spencer.

She was sent to the Institut Alpin Videmanette, an expensive finishing school in Switzerland. Young for her years and desperately homesick, she stayed there briefly before flying home again. She got a job as a teacher with Madame Vacani, the dance school so favoured by the royal family, but did not have the dedication to make a career out of it. 'She had rather a full social life,' Vacani recalled.

So she started working as a babysitter. 'She was a positive Pied Piper with children,' her mother remarked. She also worked as a daily cleaner for her sister Sarah's flatmate, Lucinda Craig-Harvey, who said: 'She dusted, she cleaned, she did the washing-up, she cleaned out the bathroom, she scrubbed the loo. And she was very good – well, good enough. She lasted a year and Sarah, as her older sister, would have got rid of her and got someone else if she hadn't been.'

It was not long before a hint of competition had crept into Diana's relationship with her sister. Sarah, initially the most attractive of the Spencer girls, enjoyed her status as the oldest in the family. It was Sarah who made the first move to London, Sarah who first attracted the attention of Prince Charles. Now her younger sister, whose looks were rapidly improving with age, was moving in on what Sarah regarded as her territory and she did not like it. It was yet another problem to add to Diana's list.

Of more importance was her relationship with her father. Diana had continued to see as much of her mother as circumstances allowed, visiting her at her home in West Sussex and, later, on the thousand-acre sheep farm she bought with Shand Kydd on the isle of Sill off Scotland's west coast, and staying with her at her home in Chelsea when she first moved to London. It was Johnny, however, who was the pivot of her life.

Johnny and Frances never recovered from the bitterness of their divorce; there was inevitable and sometimes blatant rivalry between them for the affection of their children, which meant that they showered them with more presents than was good for them. It was a contest in which – in Diana's case at least – Johnny emerged victorious. Diana adored her father, whom she perceived as a warm and kindly man who had given her the devotion of which she always felt herself in such urgent need.

Diana Spencer with Souffle, a Shetland pony, at her mother's home in Scotland during the summer of 1974

'A child is not only emotionally bonded to its parents but also chemically bonded,' said Erin Pizzey. The bitterness of the divorce – and the ferocity of her father's treatment of her mother – was submerged in her youthful subconscious. 'With a violent parent the relationship is emotionally intense and life for the child is fraught with drama. In later life the child recreates the drama of childhood.'

'There is a thing called the Spencer temper,' Charles Althorp admitted. 'We are renowned for having a very bad temper. But, at the same time, in adversity I hope that we are fairly solid and calm.'

When Diana was 15 years old Johnny Spencer fell in love and found someone to take the place of his long-departed wife. Her name was Raine. She was the daughter of Barbara Cartland, the romantic novelist whose rose-tinted view of human relations Diana was so addicted to. She also happened to be married to the Earl of Dartmouth, an old friend of Johnny's since their days at Eton. For the second time in less than a decade Spencer became involved in a messy divorce case.

Diana and her sisters never took to Raine. They resented her airs and graces, and the way she took charge of their father's life. The first time she came to lunch gave a foretaste of the squabbles to come. Mary Clarke said: 'I remember feeling tense and trying to distract Diana without success. Sarah was sent from the room and Diana followed her. We did not lunch again with Lady Dartmouth.'

When Raine eventually left her husband in 1976 after 28 years of marriage and moved in with Johnny, Sarah coldly remarked: 'Since my grandfather died last June and we moved from Sandringham to Althorp Park, Lady Dartmouth has been an all too frequent visitor.'

The teenaged children would sing 'Raine, Raine, go away'. She didn't. Two months after her divorce, Raine married Earl Spencer in a five-minute ceremony at Caxton Hall register office in central London and became chatelaine of Althorp.

The battle lines were drawn, and when Raine started selling off family treasures and redecorating the house according to her sometimes gaudy taste, the hostility between the two camps became almost palpable. The row would rumble on for the rest of Johnny Spencer's life.

'No step-relationships are easy,' he once observed. 'It was hard on my children and hard on Raine, moving into a family as close as we are. You couldn't expect it to work wonders at the start.' Or at the finish, as it happened. Charles, who inherited the house and the earldom on the death of his father in 1992, felt that an important part of his birthright had been sold off.

Diana's sense of loss was more subjective. The product of a broken home, she had focused her affections on her father. Now he had married a strong-willed woman she didn't like who quickly took charge of his life. Diana, her insecurity by then firmly established, felt herself pushed into the emotional background, a gawky adolescent who felt uncomfortable, too big and out of place.

The accompaniment to this sense of rejection had been three unpleasant divorce cases. Looking at the wreckage of broken homes and bitter partings, Diana would declare: 'I'll never marry unless I really love, really love, someone. If you're not really sure you love someone, then you might get divorced. I never want to be divorced!'

A delightful portrait of Princess Anne and Captain Mark Phillips's children, taken by Norman Parkinson for Peter's fifth birthday on 15 November 1982

Peter & Zara

MOTHERHOOD WAS AN inconvenience to the future Princess Royal. Anne resented being pregnant because it curtailed her riding activities. She heartily disliked the fuss. And by her own admission, she 'wasn't particularly keen on children'.

'Being pregnant is a very boring nine months,' she said. 'I am not particularly maternal,' she continued, adding, in her typically matter-of-fact way, 'It's an occupational hazard of being a wife.'

When on 15 November 1977, a day after her fourth wedding anniversary, she gave birth to a 7lb 9oz son in the Lindo Wing of St Mary's Hospital, Paddington, she didn't feel an overwhelming rush of 'mother love'. Her lack of enthusiasm over the baby was compensated for by her husband, Captain Mark Phillips, who was with her throughout her labour – and by the Queen.

When Her Majesty heard of the birth of her first grandchild she was about to conduct an investiture. The baby was born at 10.46am and the investiture was scheduled to start at 11am, but she was so overjoyed that she delayed the ceremony for an unprecedented ten minutes while she regained her composure. Prince Philip, who was in Germany, was equally pleased. He admired his forthright daughter and had always been very close to her. He was convinced motherhood would soften her edges and give her another dimension to her life.

Peter Mark Andrew Phillips, as the baby was to be known, was fifth in line to the throne and the first royal baby to be born to a commoner for 500 years.

Anne, who firmly believes she is a princess only by accident of birth, was adamant she would not accept titles for her children. It was for that reason that Mark refused the Queen's offer of an earldom. The Princess has always rejected the idea of ennoblement for reasons other than notable achievement and disapproved of Antony Armstrong-Jones's elevation to the earldom of Snowdon after his marriage to Princess Margaret in 1960. Everything about Anne and Mark's domestic life was calculated to distance them from the 'royal' aspect of their lives and in spite of the Queen's pleadings Anne stood firm.

She nourished the ambition that her children should be able to take up whatever career they wanted, without always being dogged by their royal heritage.

Commoner or not, Peter had – and still has – a special place in his grandmother's heart. Normally undemonstrative, the Queen was always picking him up, much to the amusement of her staff, who had never seen her touching anything other than her dogs with such outward affection.

Anne and Mark's no-nonsense approach to their firstborn reflected itself in their choice of godparents for his christening on 22 December in the Music Room at Buckingham Palace. Apart from his uncle, Prince Charles, they were close friends: Captain Hamish Lochare and the Right Reverend Geoffrey Tiarks on Mark's side; Lady Cecil Cameron and former equestrienne Jane Bullen, now Mrs Timothy Holderness-Roddam, on Anne's.

Back at Gatcombe Park, the Gloucestershire home the Queen gave them as a wedding gift, the warren of attic rooms had been transformed into a nursery suite with its own bedrooms, bathrooms, sitting room and kitchen. The furniture, mostly from the old nursery wing at Sandringham, was comfortable and cosy.

Royal nanny Mabel Anderson arrived in early 1978. Mabel, whose duties at Buckingham Palace were virtually over, had been asked by the Queen if she would like to help look after baby Peter and establish a proper nursery for Anne. Her appearance, along with the sound of her Roberts radio tuned to Terry Wogan on Radio 2, completed the familiar picture.

She soon established her routine and, apart from having to lay the nursery table for meals instead of having her own footman do it, seemed to adapt to country life. It was a young, happy household where even the butler wore jeans and Wellington boots stood in silent formation in the stone-flagged hall alongside the pram.

Anne's less than notable fervour for motherhood did not mean she was not a good mother; quite the reverse. She just approached motherhood differently from someone such as the Princess of Wales.

'The assumption that everyone wants a child and will love it from the moment it is born is responsible for a great deal of unhappiness,' child psychologist Penelope Leach observed.

Anne agreed. 'You don't actually have to like children very much to be interested in giving them the best possible start in life,' she said. And one way to achieve that was by having Mabel there. If Anne didn't have the patience or the will to play the devoted mother, she was intelligent and shrewd enough to allow someone else to do the job for her.

During the next four years Anne experienced all the usual and some of the more unusual difficulties associated with working mothers. Her seemingly limitless energy enabled her to juggle her time between her child, her husband and her increasing number of royal engagements with great dexterity.

'Whether I'm getting the balance right or nor I'm not sure,' she said. 'It's too early to say. I've been a princess all my life, but I've become a wife and mother comparatively recently.'

When the occasion demanded, Anne was wife and mother first. At harvest time, for instance, she put aside her royal duties and stayed at home. Everyone, including the household staff, helped in the fields, while Peter trotted about on the fat pony he had been given. Prince Edward and sometimes Prince Andrew would come along to spend the days in the fields and the evenings around Mabel's nursery fire, which she insisted be kept burning even if it were 80 degrees outside. It was as if nothing had ever changed.

'It was very informal,' a former member of the household remembered. 'It was a smart farmhouse that just happened to have a princess living in it.'

When Peter was three years old, Anne found she was expecting another baby. Mark was relieved; during their seven-year marriage they had stayed together by staying apart and he hoped the baby would bring them closer. So did the Queen when they told her at a belated 50th birthday party for Princess Margaret at London's Ritz Hotel. News of royal babies travels fast and the following morning Buckingham Palace was inundated with telephone calls. There was only one problem: Mark Phillips's parents didn't know.

Anne was close to her mother-in-law and anxious for her to hear the news before she read about it. The difficulty was that Anne Phillips and her husband, Peter, were on holiday in a remote Cornish cottage without a telephone. Eventually Anne contacted the local police to ask if they would send someone round with a message to telephone her. The communication got through, and shortly afterwards a worried Mrs Phillips was on the line from a callbox.

'What is it?' she asked.

'Thank goodness I reached you,' Princess Anne replied. 'I'm pregnant!'

The Queen with her first grandchild on the balcony at Buckingham Palace after the 1980 Birthday Parade

OPPOSITE PAGE: Peter Phillips cries loudly at his post-christening photocall on 22 December 1977

On 15 May 1981 at 8.15am, again in the Lindo Wing of St Mary's Hospital, Anne gave birth to a baby girl. She weighed 8lb 1oz and was delivered by the Queen's gynaecologist, George Pinker. That evening, in the decidely unglamorous surroundings of the fourth-floor wing, the Queen took her first granddaughter from her Perspex cot beside Anne's bed and held her. Like her brother, the baby had no title but was sixth in the line of succession.

In contrast to her feelings after the birth of her first child, Anne was besotted with her daughter. Guests were dragged off to see the baby in her cot or Anne would wheel the pram around the garden whilst chatting to them. Because of what the Princess describes as 'her somewhat positive arrival',

they named the baby Zara, meaning 'bright as the dawn'. According to Anne it was Prince Charles who thought of the name when he visited her in hospital and she told him about the infant's early and noisy entrance into the world. Her other names were Anne, after Mark's mother, and Elizabeth, after the Queen.

Godparents were again selected from their closest friends, and apart from Prince Andrew included no royal relations. Colonel Andrew Parker Bowles, who lived nearby with his wife, Camilla, and equestrian Hugh Thomas, who had been in the 1976 Olympic team with Anne, were the other godfathers; the Countess of Lichfield and former world champion racing driver Jackie Stewart's wife Helen, the godmothers.

Peter's parents take him for a ride on his Shetland pony Smokey at Sandringham on New Year's Day 1981

OPPOSITE PAGE: Anne and Mark with their firstborn at Gatcombe Park in July 1980

Two months before Zara was born, nanny Mabel Anderson decided it was time for retirement. She had fulfilled her promise and brought up Peter Phillips – and coped with the informality of Gatcombe, to which she never totally adapted. The absence of a nursery footman, a nursery maid and her own chauffeur had not deterred her unduly, but she felt a second baby would be too much.

Mabel's life had revolved around royal children for 33 years; it was time to fold away her stiffly starched uniform. South Africa beckoned and Mabel handed over the nursery reins to northerner Pat Moss, who was brought in not to take over but to share the duties with her royal employer, who started taking a decidedly unroyal practical interest in her children.

If anyone had told her she would actually enjoy changing nappies and prefer to be bathing a baby than out riding, Anne would probably have told them to 'naff off', but Zara had stirred her maternal instincts. It did not mean she loved Peter any less; it was simply that she felt more protective about Zara.

As the children got older and their childish pranks more naughty, it was Anne who dished out the discipline. She was stricter than Mark, though not obsessively so. If the children were noisy when they should have been quiet she would shout and tell them to shut up, but she did not mind their childish mess or when Peter clambered on top of the piano in his Wellingtons.

If they did irritate her, however, she had no qualms about slapping them – even in public – and packing them off to bed.

The Queen, who loved having the duo to stay, was equally firm. She might have been a doting granny but she was a strict one too.

LEFT: Peter and Zara with Nanny Pat Moss *en route* to Balmoral via Aberdeen railway station on 5 August 1982

OPPOSITE PAGE: Princess Anne takes her daughter to the 1983 Burghley Horse Trials in Lincolnshire

'She was always chastising them,' a rating on board *Britannia* remembered. 'I've seen her shake Zara when she's been naughty.'

Something which did indeed happen when once Zara was running up and down stairs, and continued to do so despite being told by the Queen not to do so.

On Nanny's day off, Anne would look after the children. She would go upstairs in the morning to wake them, then dress them and prepare them a cooked breakfast. If it were a weekday either Anne's policeman or Mark would then take them to school, while Anne made the beds and tidied up the nursery.

If it were a weekend they would all go riding together, staying up in the stable yard until lunchtime. Mark would take over when they came home, playing hide-and-seek or rolling about with them on the floor. He had no qualms about playing childish games or teaching them to ride. Nor did Anne.

From the start, the Princess refused to be influenced by public opinion in the way she brought up her children. 'If you start down that road there's no end to it,' she said. 'You must do what you think is best for your child.' As a farmer's wife that meant country pursuits and country schools.

And so it was that Queen Elizabeth II's first grandchild, a great-great-grandson of King George V, began his education, not with a governess in the peaceful atmosphere of the Buckingham Palace schoolroom but at a nursery school in nearby Minchinhampton.

Zara followed him there and fitted in so well that for a time the other mothers did not realise who she was. Staff were at pains not to single Zara out as someone special. 'I treat Zara just like all the others,' the headmistress said.

'She is a lovely little girl and just like any other child of her age she can be a rascal. She has made lots of friends and is very popular and she really enjoys learning.'

Like most four-year-old girls her favourite lessons were music and movement, and the only hint that there was something different about her was the presence of one of the ubiquitous royal detectives. Zara followed Peter to Blueboys School in the same town. She stayed there until its closure in 1989, when Anne moved her to the upmarket Beaudesert prep school. By this time Pat Moss had left and been replaced by a less traditional nanny, Sarah Minty, who helped around the house and on the farm when the children were at school.

'I think the Queen found this rather alarming,' says a former member of the household, 'but Anne wanted to deal with the children herself.'

'You've got to be completely objective as far as children are concerned,' Anne explained. 'Consider the personality of your child and try to work out what's going to be the right thing for him or for her at the end of the day.'

BELOW: The Phillips siblings with their cousin Prince William for the flypast that followed the Trooping the Colour ceremony on 16 June 1984

OPPOSITE PAGE: Eight-year-old Peter wears a suit and tie for a service at St George's Chapel, Windsor, on 21 April 1986 to mark the Queen's 60th birthday

The right thing for Peter and Zara, Anne and Mark decided, was a co-educational prep school. Port Regis, near Shaftesbury in Dorset. Both parents felt the school suited the strong personalities of their children. Peter started there as a boarder aged seven, and Zara four years later, when she was eight. The Phillipses liked the headmaster, David Pritchard, whose ideas on bringing up children were similar to their own.

Despite her royal duties – Princess Anne undertook 84 royal engagements the year Zara was born and some 168 the year after, plus an extensive Save the Children charity trek – she still found time to be with her children.

Her extraordinary physical energy allowed her to work all day, get home, change into jeans, cook supper for the children and then help with their homework without turning a hair (not that that would ever have worried the fashion-unconscious Princess).

While Mark snoozed in front of the television, Anne struggled to help Peter and Zara with their prep. 'To try to help my children to read was actually very difficult,' she confessed. 'I was concerned that I was doing them a disfavour, because my logic worked differently from theirs.'

Whatever skills they lacked in the schoolroom, Peter and Zara made up for outside. They both learnt to ride as soon as they could walk and by the age of four were quite capable of managing without a leading rein. Their life revolved around country pursuits and at weekends, instead of being left behind with Nanny, they went with their parents wherever they were going.

Sometimes they misbehaved and sometimes their mischief made headlines, as when Peter – much to his mother's silent amusement – turned on the pursuing photographers and yelled at them.

'Shove off, you *******,' he is reported to have said to one, but no one could confirm if it was Master Phillips in full cry or one of his friends.

When the children joined Gatcombe Park shooting parties, their presence caused criticism amongst anti-bloodsport groups. One year Peter, then aged seven and carrying a toy pistol of his own, swung a dead pheasant round and tossed it into the air. Five years later Zara, dressed in a miniature Barbour jacket and wellies, was helping to pick up dead birds when she discovered an injured one.

Not having a gun with which to kill it, she used her foot to put the bird out of its misery. Once again the League Against Cruel Sports spoke out. The headline ran: ANNE'S GIRL STOMPS ON PHEASANT'S HEAD! Anne took no notice.

The royal family, like most country people, take a fatalistic view of the balance between man and nature. Dealing with guns and dying birds was regarded simply as part of their training. And while Zara was not all sweetness – she could be a 'bossy little madam', one of the staff recalled – she was not cruel. She was just being brought up a country girl as her parents wanted.

Living in the rural retreat of Gloucestershire did not stop Zara from enjoying dressing up, and when the Queen gave her granddaughter special permission to attend the Royal Ascot meeting in June 1989, the eight-year-old proudly wore a blue spotted dress with a straw hat, carried a tiny handbag and looked immensely pleased with her 'grown-up' self.

In the days before Zara and Peter formed firm friendships of their own, they saw a lot of their cousins, William and Harry. Gatcombe Park is not far from the Waleses' country home, Highgrove, and Diana would ensure the children had tea together every few weeks, especially if Anne was away.

When the Waleses' entourage was due at Gatcombe everyone was apprehensive. The little Princes would arrive followed by a back-up car and two detectives, looking, as one guest observed, 'as if they were going to a party in Belgravia', with carefully pressed shorts and shiny leather shoes. The boys greeted Anne's offer of a trip to the stables with enthusiasm; less so their mother, who never managed to bring their Wellingtons. For all Diana's efforts, however, William and Harry would always return to Highgrove as dishevelled and muddy as boys like to be.

When the Prince and Princess of Wales came over, which they occasionally did for a shooting weekend or birthday party, the house was thrown into turmoil. Three back-up cars with armed police would race up the drive and when they arrived no one was sure what to do. Charles was very particular and everything in his bedroom had to be just right or he made a fuss. He had no time for Mark and was rather awkward with his godson, Peter.

'He was bemused by children,' a member of staff remembered. 'He was not a natural like Mark Phillips. Instead he would try and be funny in that Goonish sort of way that children don't respond to. He would affect strange voices which would tend to frighten them rather than encourage them to play.'

In the Eighties, one of Anne and Mark's guests was unable to join the shoot and they were racking their brains to think of a local substitute they knew well enough to ask at the last minute.

'What about Wales?' someone helpfully suggested.

'Oh no!' Anne said, 'He's far too grand.'

'Too grand?' the perplexed guest piped up. 'But you had the Queen and the Duke of Edinburgh last weekend.'

'The trouble is,' the Princess said, 'the Queen and the Duke of Edinburgh aren't grand and Charles is.'

In spite of all their differences, brother and sister get on well and were supportive of each other during their respective marital problems. But like her father, Anne has little time for the minutiae of protocol. She also has the self-confidence of her father and, knowing how important it is, has tried her best to develop it in her children.

Her no-nonsense approach to motherhood meant she treated them as mini-adults. She taught them to enjoy the things she enjoyed like riding, sailing and shooting. She also impressed upon them the importance of good manners, though, like their mother, they did not always reach the exacting standards set for them. And she tried to work out what was best for them.

'The child must come first,' she said.

She believes that a child's home life has a greater influence on it than school and, like Prince Charles, believes in the importance of parental example. Even during the height of their marital discord, Anne and Mark tried to adhere to that creed. They never rowed about their children and they never rowed in front of their children. They tried to be the ideal parents, but they weren't the ideal couple.

When Anne first discussed the possibility of a separation with the Queen, her mother's first concern was her grandchildren. She couldn't understand why Anne couldn't stick it out, as she had done herself for so many years. The Queen liked Mark – she admired his horsemanship – and Prince Philip saw him as an achiever. Until Prince Charles married in 1981, Mark's parents were always invited to Windsor for the Christmas celebrations. Anne Phillips and the Queen had more in common than just their grandchildren and the two women would meet at Chelsea Flower Show and dine at Buckingham Palace afterwards.

Princess Anne was not to be swayed, however, and the couple

were divorced in 1992. They made every effort, nonetheless, to remain on amicable terms for the sake of their children and put on a show of togetherness when the occasion demanded.

In September 1991, for instance, when Peter started at what is now the royal family's alma mater, Gordonstoun, his parents drove him there and spent almost three hours at the school before leaving in separate cars. Peter, who had already displayed his prowess at sport, settled in well – certainly better than his uncle Charles.

The divorce did not cause any noticeable disruption in Zara and Peter's life. They had been brought up with a father who was abroad on business frequently and a mother whose royal duties and work for Save the Children Fund took her away from home for long periods. And when they were all together, Anne and Mark always made an effort to shield their children from their own problems.

When Anne married Timothy Laurence in December 1992 they appeared to adapt well to this change in their domestic circumstances.

The only real difference now was that their father, instead of living in the big house with them, was based nearby at Aston Farm, two miles away, but still part of the 730-acre Gatcombe estate. Peter and Zara continued to see as much of their father as before. He had unlimited access to them and they joined him for as many holidays as his work schedule permitted.

Anne's efforts to keep her children out of the limelight, while letting them know the limelight was there, seemed to pay dividends. Perhaps it was too early to judge, she conceded, but there was enough evidence to suggest that you don't have to be someone who has always yearned for children in order to be a good mother – and that a rigid and lonely regime is not the only way for a princess to raise her children.

LEFT: Princess Anne explains the course to her children before a charity showjumping event at Ascot in July 1987

OPPOSITE PAGE: Peter and Zara are prepared for the rain and mud at horse trials near Chippenham, Wiltshire, in 1986

William & Harry

DIANA WAS A tactile mother, forever embracing and cuddling her sons; she held their hands and vowed they would never suffer the kind of childhood she did. She was a product of what is now known as a dysfunctional family, the survivor of emotional abuse, which according to today's psychologists is a very real form of child abuse. She was determined that William and Harry would never lie in their beds frightened, lonely and confused, as she had.

'A child's stability arises mainly from the affection received from their parents, and there is no substitute for affection,' she once said. Whatever happened in her rapidly changing world, they came first.

In that she was like millions of other young mothers with two lively and occasionally naughty boys to contend with. She missed them 'like mad' when they were away at school, wrote to them at least twice a week and longed for their misspelled Sunday letters in return, with their schoolboy lack of detail. And she resolutely stuck to her avowed intention – to bring up her children in as 'ordinary' a way as possible.

Unlike her mother-in-law, who also had the same intention but whose definition of the word was always circumscribed by her royal position, 'ordinary' meant precisely that.

Diana was not raised in a palace surrounded by courtiers. Her childhood was most certainly privileged, but it was not constrained by that suffocating commitment to appearances and form that marked royal as opposed to aristocratic upbringings. She had been allowed to make friends and get dirty; to show emotion, to cry (indeed, there were times when it had been hard to stem the tears); to pursue her interests to the best of her abilities.

For all Prince Philip's innovations, the ghost of old Queen Mary still seemed to be stalking the corridors of Buckingham Palace, watching over her royal descendants. Diana was only three and a half weeks past her 20th birthday when she married Prince Charles at St Paul's Cathedral that summer morning in July 1981. She belonged to another world, and would find it difficult to come to terms with life as a member of the royal family. Her relationship with her husband would cause her enormous and very public problems. On matters pertaining to her children, however, Diana was insistent on having her own way, right from the start.

OPPOSITE PAGE: The Prince and Princess of Wales pose for a family portrait with sons William and Harry in October 1984

By tradition royal babies were born at home, usually a royal one. But Diana, like Anne, broke with convention. William was born in the private Lindo Wing of St Mary's Hospital in Paddington. His mother had her own room, but it was neither large nor luxurious. The bed was standard hospital issue. The walls were covered with dull floral-patterned paper. And though she had windows on two sides of her room, the view, out over rooftops and down on to a back street, could not be called scenic. The bathroom was across the hallway.

That was the way Diana wanted it. Her doctor, George Pinker, surgeon-gynaecologist to the Queen, did not subscribe to home births. And Betty Parsons, who helped thousands of women in childbirth with her relaxation techniques and assisted the Queen at the birth of Prince Edward, held that if complications were to arise a hospital was the best place to deal with them. That was a good enough argument for Diana, and on 21 June 1982 she was duly delivered of a son weighing 7lb 1½ oz.

'He has a wisp of fair hair, sort of blondish, and blue eyes,' Prince Charles proudly told the crowd waiting outside.

Diana was back there two years later to give birth to Prince Harry.

They were not easy confinements. Diana, like many first-time mothers, believed in 'natural' childbirth. William's arrival changed her view; after several hours in labour she had to be given an epidural injection to relieve the pain. Harry's birth, his father remarked, was 'much quicker'. Even so, it still took nine hours, which prompted Diana to say 'If men had babies they would only have one each.'

The results were worth the effort, though, and Diana – still a child herself in many ways – took pride and maternal comfort in her sons. Seeking compensation for the lack of stability and affection in her own childhood, she was intent on building a secure and loving home for her children. Charles respected this. Raised in a matriarchal family, always closer to his mother than his father, the Prince of Wales had decidedly old-fashioned views on a wife's duty.

'Although the whole attitude has changed towards what women are expected to do, I still feel, all the same, at the risk of sticking my neck out, that one of the most important roles any woman could ever perform is to be a mother,' he said.

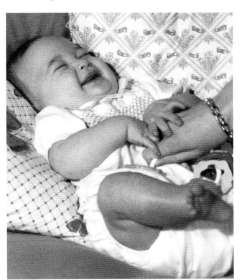

'Nobody should denigrate that role. How children grow up, what attitudes they have, are absolutely vital both from the social point of view and for the future. And all this stems so much from the role the mother performs. I know it's awfully difficult nowadays because women want to work and have to do so, to earn enough. But the role of the mother is so terribly important.'

From the beginning, Diana was determined to exert her authority in the upbringing of William and Harry. If she did not do so, she knew she would lose them to a system she neither liked nor understood. She was, however, still very much a newcomer to royalty and had to tread warily. The choice of godparents for William was very much Charles's – Princess Alexandra; the Queen's lady-in-waiting, Lady Susan Hussey; ex-King Constantine of Greece; Lord Romsey, grandson of Earl Mountbatten; the South African mystic Sir Laurens van der Post, in whose philosophy and storytelling ability Charles placed such great store; and the Duke of Westminster's wife, Tally, the only one of the six who was anywhere near Diana's age.

When it came to Harry, however, Diana insisted on having the final say, and his godparents were Carolyn Bartholomew; Princess Margaret's daughter, Lady Sarah Armstrong-Jones; Cece, Lord Vestey's second wife; Prince Andrew; old Etonian farmer Gerald Ward; and the artist Bryan Organ, who had painted Diana in 1981.

Charles was an enthusiastic father at the beginning. A child, he mused, in the manner of Laurens van der Post, 'is the culmination of who knows how many thousands of years and the genetic make-up of your ancestors'. He read copiously on the subject of how best to bring up children, including Betty Parsons' amusing guide, *The Expectant Father*, which advised him how to help and encourage his wife.

Always on the lookout for some guiding truth, gradually the Prince's own theories developed.

ABOVE: Six-month-old William of Wales chuckles as his mother (unseen) tickles his tummy during a photocall at Kensington Palace

OPPOSITE PAGE: The Prince with his parents, maternal grandparents and great-grandmother after his christening at Buckingham Palace on 4 August 1982

'I would like to try and bring up our children to be well-mannered, to think of other people, to put themselves in other people's positions, to do unto others as they would have done to them,' he said. 'That way, even if they turn out to be not very bright or very qualified, at least if they have reasonable manners they will get so much further in life than if they did not have any at all.'

Charles seemed to be implying that intelligence and qualifications were of secondary importance, and in a sense they are. The royal family is judged on the way it conducts itself on public occasions, not by its academic prowess. To be able to stand still for hours on end, to make small talk with strangers, to appear dignified in even the most undignified of situations is more important, as Queen Mary astutely pointed out, than an ability to pass a bookkeeping exam. To acquire those requisite royal manners – 'simple, old-fashioned values for survival', as Charles called them – takes training of a disciplined, old-fashioned sort associated with a traditional British nanny.

BELOW: Barbara Barnes carries William down the aircraft steps after a 27-hour flight from New Zealand, where in 1983 his parents were on an official tour

William waves to the crowd outside St Mary's Hospital, Paddington, after seeing newborn brother Harry for the first time, September 1984

OPPOSITE PAGE: Diana and Charles show their nine-month-old son to the media in the grounds of Government House in Auckland, 23 April 1983

'There are some experts who were very certain about how you should bring up children,' Charles said. 'But then, after 20 years, they turned round and said they'd been wrong. Think of all the poor people who had followed their suggestions.'

One of those experts was Diana's distant relation, Dr Benjamin Spock, the most influential advocate of the new permissive attitude towards childcare. He would later recant many of his theories. By then, however, his *Common Sense Book of Unity and Child Care*, first published in 1946, had become the authoritative home reference work, its call for a closer, more-compliant relationship between parent and child the accepted orthodoxy even amongst people who had never read it. And Diana was one of those 'poor people' who had every intention of doing exactly what Spock had advised.

The arguments between husband and wife started almost as soon as William was born. Charles wanted to name his son Arthur Albert. Diana objected and the child was christened William Arthur Philip Louis instead. On the subject of nannies she was also adamant. Her own experience with them had left her with unhappy memories. 'A mother's arms are so much more comforting than anyone else's,' she said.

Prince Charles had wanted to employ his old nanny, Mabel Anderson, who along with Helen Lightbody had played such a significant role in his young life. Diana quickly vetoed the suggestion. Mabel, the Princess argued, was too old and too traditional.

If she had to have someone – and it was pointed out to her that because of other public duties she needed someone to help her look after the children – it would be someone of *her* choice, someone who agreed with *her* ideas.

Charles, keen to do what his valet called with exaggeration 'anything for a quiet life', gave way, and Barbara Barnes was duly hired. She was the first royal nanny not to have at least two footmen and two housemaids to help her.

'I'm here to help the Princess, not to take over,' Barbara declared tactfully.

FROM FAR LEFT: Prince William, ten days away from his second birthday, at play in the garden at Kensington Palace

Diana looks on as Jane Mynors greets William on his first day at her nursery school in west London, 24 September 1985

The Princess of Wales and baby Harry board the Royal Yacht in Portsmouth on 7 August 1985 for the annual Western Isles cruise

Grumpy-looking William and his parents ride through Windsor in a carriage after a service to celebrate the Queen's 60th birthday, 21 April 1986

The daughter of a forestry worker, Barbara came to the Waleses on the recommendation of her previous employer, Colin Tennant, later Lord Glenconner, whose wife, Anne, was a lady-in-waiting to Princess Margaret. Calm and capable, she had an easy manner that children responded to and she got on extremely well with her young charges. Possibly too well, for one of Diana's less laudable characteristics was her jealousy. Always possessive, she secretly came to envy the early rapport Charles established with his sons.

Charles had revived the ritual of bath-time and, unlike his mother, who used to sit majestically on her chair to view the proceedings from a splash-free distance, Charles made a point of joining William for his evening bath to encourage him to get used to it. One night when they were both due to go out for an engagement, Diana couldn't find Charles anywhere. She eventually discovered him in the bath with William.

They were having a great time,' she said. 'There was soap and water everywhere.'

Diana approved, for a time. As the difficulties in her marriage developed into a chasm, she came to regard her husband as a poor father and those moments of tenderness as nothing more than paternal window-dressing. 'Charles knows so much about babies, he can have the next one,' she once remarked irritably.

That was unfair. He did not find it easy to communicate with young children who respond to the person, not the position, and his Goonish jokes and funny faces frightened as often as they amused. With his own kin, however, he established an intimacy he had never enjoyed in any relationship and he derived immense pleasure from it. It was Diana he had the problem with.

Around the same time her relationship with Nanny Barnes started to fray. Not in any obvious way, but the atmosphere at the Waleses' London home, Kensington Palace, changed. Diana wanted her sons to herself and came to see Barbara as a potential rival for their affections. A feeling of tension crept in.

The parting came shortly after Barbara had flown to the West Indies just before Christmas 1986 for the 60th birthday party Lord Glenconner gave for himself on his private island, Mustique. She was photographed enjoying herself in the company of such fellow revellers as Princess Margaret, Jerry Hall and Raquel Welch.

Charles, as a defensive mechanism designed to safeguard his own sense of dignity, had become something of a stickler for the finer observances of royal protocol. 'He will not sit down at a table unless it is correctly laid,' a member of staff revealed. 'If there is a speck of dust on the cream, for instance,

he will ring the bell and have it taken away. He is waited on hand and foot in a way that is almost obscene.' In this cloistered world nannies had their place and it was not being photographed on a beach in the West Indies.

He also became irked at the way people would compliment his nanny, as if he had nothing to do with his sons' manners and generally personable behaviour.

In the end it was Nanny herself who decided that it would be better for all concerned if she left. On 15 January 1987 it was announced that Barbara Barnes would be leaving royal employ. The statement was timed to coincide with William's first day at his new school. 'I thought no one would notice,' Diana later said, 'but I was wrong, wasn't I?' She was.

The British press, sensing a story, put the news of Barbara's departure on page one and relegated William's arrival at pre-preparatory school to the inside pages. In fact the parting, all speculation to the contrary notwithstanding, was amicable.

Barbara had been consulted about her replacement and was given a grace-and-favour home in south London. She continued to exchange Christmas and birthday cards with the Waleses and their sons. She left simply because her term of employment had run its course and William's arrival at Wetherby in west London had seemed the appropriate moment to make the break.

The young Prince had already had a taste of life on the other side of the palace walls and in that Diana had taken the lead. When she visited Young England kindergarten in Pimlico, where she worked before her marriage, William had been dispatched to play with the other children. They were playing 'Galloping Horses', but he did not know how to join in that game of putting one foot in front of the other and clip-clopping around the room. Incidents like that convinced Diana, as sensitive as her son to any feeling of being 'different', that he would greatly benefit from mixing with others of his own age.

Young England was too far away so Mrs Mynors' nursery school in nearby Notting Hill was selected. 'His classmates hardly know who he is,' Mrs Mynors suggested.

That was not strictly true. He was soon informing his classmates, 'My daddy's a real prince.' And in a fit of temper, he once threatened an adversary with 'all the Queen's horses and men'.

RIGHT: Prince Harry, a Thomas the Tank Engine bag tucked under his arm, waves to photographers on his first day at kindergarten, 16 September 1987

OPPOSITE PAGE: Brother William is a rather fidgety attendant at the wedding of Prince Andrew to Sarah Ferguson in Westminster Abbey in July 1986

For William and, later, Harry to have been kept in ignorance of their position was simply an impossibility. The escort of protection officers, the palaces and the subservient attitude of those who came into contact with their parents inevitably made an impression on their young minds. As one member of staff pointed out, 'There is nothing normal about those children; there is nothing normal about having two back-up cars wherever you go.'

Nor was that awareness to be entirely discouraged. However 'ordinary' their parents might wish their sons' childhoods to be, they were royal, and the best way to learn how to deal with that was from the earliest possible age. As their mother's adjustment problems testified.

But if their future was unquestioned, the manner of their education was not. There was consultation. In the end, though, it was Diana who had the deciding voice. 'She is very good at getting her own way,' her father observed.

William and Harry were not first taught at home by a governess, but instead started their education at a nursery school. They then went to Wetherby and on to Ludgrove, a preparatory boarding school in Berkshire where Henry Hansell, who was tutor to George V's children, was once a master. They did not attend Cheam, Charles's old school, and Diana argued vehemently against Gordonstoun.

It was a clear break with royal tradition – and her husband. In the British upper classes it is almost invariably the father who makes the final decision in the choice of schools for a son. In this family the father was overruled.

As one of Diana's royal relations remarked: 'She's the strong one in the marriage, especially when it comes to the children.'

There was another sign of Diana's resolve to break free from the constraints of royal convention and that was in the all-important area of clothes. The royal family, with the loud-checked exception of the Duke of Windsor (and he was hardly an example to follow), have always been careful to eschew high fashion. Their clothes, down to the length of the women's hemlines and the cut of the men's suits, have been determinedly conservative, as befitting a family which sees itself as the guardian of conservative values.

LEFT: The Princess of Wales and her younger son at the Royal Palace in Mallorca in August 1987 during a holiday with the Spanish royal family

OPPOSITE PAGE: The Waleses prepare for a cycling trip in Tresco whilst visiting the Scilly Isles in June 1989

Diana changed that. She turned herself into a fashion plate – much to the chagrin of the palace old guard who believed that by dressing like a soap star she was devaluing the currency of majesty. But high glamour nonetheless became Diana's style and she dressed her sons to reflect it.

Abandoning the velvet-collared coats and short trousers of her husband's youth, she had them wearing striped T-shirts by Jean Bourget, sweatshirts and corduroy trousers from Benetton and Osh Kosh dungarees.

For one photo session at Sandringham in the winter of 1988 she turned out William and Harry in matching pale blue coats trimmed with white and fastened with mother-of-pearl buttons.

She had the design copied for her by Catherine Walker, but this was one occasion when her fashion sense deserted her; when she and William later appeared in their his-and-her outfits, she was exposed to exactly the kind of ridicule she always went to such pains in avoid.

Diana was on safer ground when she insisted on taking William with her to Australia when he was only a few months old. The Queen and the Queen Mother had both left their young progeny behind when they had visited the Antipodes and this separation of mother and child had become the custom. But Diana was a strong believer in 'bonding'. She refused to leave her newborn in the care of nannies as her in-laws had, and it was a wet, wailing and jet-lagged infant Prince who accompanied his parents to Woomargama in the Australian outback with a supply of food supplements, fluoride drops and multi-vitamins.

RIGHT: Harry is pleased to join his big brother at Wetherby School in Notting Hill in September 1989

OPPOSITE PAGE: William meets the public after the 1991 St David's Day service at Llandaff Cathedral

Diana's possessiveness sometimes bemused Charles, who was conditioned to put duty before family. He could share her feeling of loss when Harry followed William to Mrs Mynors'.

'It made me feel very sad – I had a big lump in my throat when we left Harry,' he said. He understood why Diana, as she put it, 'dived into the Kleenex box' when William left home to go to Ludgrove. 'It's quite something putting one's eldest into school,' the Princess wrote to a friend, 'but William seemed quite confident about everything.'

These were emotional set pieces that echoed Charles's own childhood experiences. But on general issues – how much time they should spend with their children, where to take their holidays – they were moving ever further apart. It was a sour overspill from their marital problems, and sometimes a focus for them.

William and Harry were two decidedly different characters who reacted to these strains in their own way. William, a bothersome baby much given to tears, a troublesome infant who took delight in throwing shoes into lavatories, was always portrayed as being adventurous and forceful; his brother as sweet and rather shy.

In the beginning that was true. William had always seemed the more anxious of the two to get out into life, to make friends, to make the explorations expected of a little boy, while Harry had a tendency to hang back. At Mrs Mynors' Harry had hidden in the playground and refused to join the other children in their games, and had been too embarrassed to hold up his hand in class to be 'excused' to go to the lavatory.

That changed as they grew older. Harry fought his way past the troubles in his parents' marriage to become a confident and rather mischievous boy, better at riding and skiing than his brother. 'Harry's the naughty one, just like me,' his mother said.

The younger Prince had a particular fondness for the flora and fauna of the countryside and took pleasure in his menagerie

of pets, as his mother and father did when they were young. When one of the pet ducklings he kept at Kensington Palace went missing, the worry was that it had wandered next door and been devoured by Princess Michael of Kent's cat.

One of the policemen was sent on a search and rescue mission. It was found unharmed in the care of Princess Michael's secretary.

'Harry loves animals and plants,' his father explained. Charles tried to pass on his New Age philosophy to his son. 'I tell him all about them and say they have feelings too and mustn't be hurt.'

That does not extend to the field sports so beloved by the royal family. Charles rode to hounds, stalked stags on the Balmoral estate and shot pheasants at Sandringham. It was not an interest he shared with his first wife. She was not an enthusiast. She allowed William and Harry to join the weekend shoots at Sandringham because they are such an established royal tradition, but when Anne once suggested taking the boys out shooting herself, she firmly said 'No'.

It was a decision William would not have questioned. For all his initial boisterousness, he was a sensitive youngster who intuitively picked up the tensions. He was very close to his mother.

'William is a very self-possessed, intelligent and mature boy and quite shy,' said his uncle Charles, the 9th Earl Spencer. 'He is quite formal and stiff.'

It was William who tried to take care of his mother in her moments of crisis, and Diana's friends remarked how she spoke to her elder son as if he were an adult. And how mother and son held hands and cuddled each other frequently.

'I want to bring them security,' the Princess said, explaining her approach to motherhood.

'I hug my children to death and get into bed with them at night. I always feed them love and affection – it's so important.'

RIGHT: Diana, William and Harry attend the traditional Easter Day service at St George's Chapel in April 1992

OPPOSITE PAGE: The Princess is reunited with her boys on board *Britannia* in Toronto during a tour of Canada in 1991

Especially to William and Harry, who could not help but be aware of their parents' unhappy relationship. William, being pre-adolescent, became alternately attention-seeking then introverted, consumed with the idea that his mother's unhappiness might be his fault. When she locked herself in the bathroom to cry uncontrollably, he tried to help by pushing tissues under the door.

When he was away at school, where telephone calls were not allowed, he never missed an opportunity to speak to 'Mummy'. Once during the summer of 1992, when the scandal surrounding the Princess was at its height, he begged to be allowed to use a friend's parents' mobile car phone, 'just to call Mummy'.

William tried to become what is known in psychological terms as 'a controller' – a little child, burdened with his family's distress, trying manfully to carry all the problems on his own shoulders.

Sophie Dahl, granddaughter of children's author Roald, whose own young life was scarred by similar scenes of familial conflict, says: 'To start with the publicity made me feel important because Mummy was in the newspapers. But then I started to think, "How could they do this to Mummy and why didn't Daddy protect her?"'

For William it was the hardest, cruellest training for the job he was born to inherit one day. For whatever feelings he may have had, he still had to behave in the way his position demanded.

Sometimes the strain became too much. 'I don't want to be a king,' he told a school friend that miserable summer. 'I want to be a policeman.'

RIGHT: Harry and his mother watch a parade for the 50th anniversary of VJ-Day in The Mall, 19 August 1995

OPPOSITE PAGE: The Prince rides in a tank at the barracks of the Light Dragoons in Hanover, July 1993

Both boys, however, had the good manners their father wanted, politely shaking hands, writing thank-you notes, coming down in their dressing-gowns to say goodnight to guests their parents might be entertaining at Kensington Palace or Highgrove.

There had been a few early difficulties. When Bob Geldof called at Kensington Palace to discuss the famine problem in Africa with Charles, William took one look at the perennially dishevelled Irishman and declared, 'He's all dirty. He's got scruffy hair and wet shoes.'

The iconoclastic Geldof retorted, 'Shut up, you horrible little boy. Your hair's scruffy, too.'

'No, it's not,' William replied, taken aback by the visitor's outspokenness. 'My mother brushed it.'

It was the kind of exchange William was discouraged from repeating. His nannies would not allow it. Diana's early reluctance to entrust her children to the care of someone else had been modified by necessity and after Barbara Barnes left she poached Ruth Wallace from Prince and Princess Michael of Kent. Next came Jessie Webb, who had worked for the

Duchess of York's interior decorator, Nina Campbell, for 15 years. Giving consistency to these domestic arrangements was Olga Powell, who had started as under-nanny at the same time as Barbara Barnes. All were 'old-fashioned' nannies, in the sense that they subscribed to the notions of routine and order and, of course, to the 'Ps and Qs' and the general politeness expected of any 'well brought-up' child.

As Dr Charles Lewis of Lancaster University explained: 'However fraught the parents' relationship might be, and however often they are absent from home, a loving nanny can stabilise the situation for the children and fulfil the parents' role quite happily.'

There was inconsistency in Diana's approach to discipline, however. In the early 1990s, when William was in the Royal Mews at Buckingham Palace, he was about to get into one of the carriages when he delivered a sharp kick to the leg of the footman helping him in. Diana was very angry and slapped him on the bottom. Yelling with hurt pride, William clambered inside the carriage and sat next to his mother, sobbing.

His tears made her feel so guilty she immediately picked him up and cuddled him, thus negating the punishment she had just administered.

Her wish not to spoil her sons was equally fraught with contradiction. Diana tried not to spoil them as she and her brother had been by parents who had tried to buy their affection. At Christmas they were given a Hamley's toyshop catalogue and asked to tick the presents they wanted. 'It makes you very materialistic,' Charles Spencer remembered.

But executing the good intention not to spoil her children proved very difficult for Diana. She asked her friends to give them books instead of toys, but the gifts still showered their way. Singer Barry Manilow gave Harry a valuable five-inch antique baby piano, while Jaguar presented William with a miniature motor car that he crashed into the garage wall. And when it came to things like parties, Diana, for all her good intentions, could be equally indulgent.

One year William had a tea party in the insect house at London Zoo. Smarty Arty, the entertainer much favoured by the well-to-do of London society at the time, was hired to provide the entertainment. In 1992 ex-King Constantine gave his godson a Cowboys and Indians birthday party at his north London home. Diana wore a cowgirl outfit; Charles, who is an honorary Indian chief and has the full regalia, including the leather bonnet, confined himself to a Stetson, while both William and Harry wore cowboy outfits. It was at the height of the speculation about the royal marriage, but Charles and Diana presented a united front in the presence of the children.

'You wouldn't have thought anything was the matter,' said Smarty Arty, who was there to organise the games, dressed as a big fat cowboy. They joined in all the games like running with a plate of water and appeared to be thoroughly enjoying themselves.

At another fancy-dress party, this time at Christmas, William dressed as Michael Jackson while brother Harry went as a Ninja Turtle, complete with shell.

Although Charles and Diana attended these family celebrations together, the problems in their marriage were never far away. She tried to arrange her schedule to fit in with her children; he would not cancel an engagement or alter an arrangement and sometimes chose to stay away from home for weeks on end.

And as they grew ever further apart, an element of what looked like malice crept into their relationship. She would go out of her way to upstage him. He in turn allegedly took cold delight in upsetting her.

When Sergeant Barry Mannakee, her former bodyguard, to whom she had grown particularly fond, was killed in a motorcycle accident, Charles did not tell her straight away. He waited until the car that was taking them to an official engagement came to a halt. Then, just as she was opening the door, he said, 'Mannakee's dead!' and pushed her out.

Such incidents only heightened their conflict, which came to a public head when William was rushed to hospital in 1991.

ABOVE: Prince William, in distinctive Eton College uniform for the first time, sets off for lessons, 6 September 1995

OPPOSITE PAGE: The second in line to the throne arrives at the school the previous afternoon with his parents and younger brother

A group of boys, accompanied by a master, were walking along carrying golf clubs when the lad in front of William swung his club over his shoulder, catching the Prince full on the temple. Without having time to press the emergency bleeper on his wrist, William fell to the ground, blood pouring from his head. No one knew how badly he was hurt and Graham, his detective, put the emergency plan into action, alerting the Royal Berkshire Hospital then the Princess of Wales.

Within minutes William was in an ambulance on his way to hospital in nearby Reading. Transferred to Great Ormond Street Hospital for Sick Children in London, he was operated on under general anaesthetic for a depressed fracture of the skull.

Charles and Diana had hurried to his bedside – she from a lunch at San Lorenzo restaurant in Knightsbridge, he from Highgrove. Diana insisted on staying at the hospital during the operation. Charles left to attend a performance of Puccini's opera, *Tosca*, at Covent Garden where he entertained a party of European Union officials. It was, he insisted, his duty — and in the royal family duty always comes before any personal consideration. Diana was appalled by what she saw as his

Charles and Harry enjoy a toboggan ride in the Swiss ski resort of Klosters, January 1997

OPPOSITE PAGE: William at Windsor Castle after his confirmation on 9 March 1997. *Left to right*: **Prince Harry, Diana, Princess of Wales, Prince William, the Prince of Wales and the Queen.** *Back row*: **godparents King Constantine, Lady Susan Hussey, Princess Alexandra, the Duchess of Westminster and Lord Romsey**

callous indifference to the plight of their son. He accused her of overstating the severity of the injury – of playing the role, not of princess but of drama queen. The British public appeared to take Diana's side. *The Sun*, in one blazing headline, summed up the argument that raged in the newspapers for several days afterwards: 'What kind of dad are you?' it asked. Not a very good one, the newspaper concluded.

Once he was better, William enjoyed the attention showered on him. He accompanied his mother to Wimbledon – he and Harry had tennis lessons from former champion Steffi Graf –

and was allowed to invite out whoever he liked from school. Unlike his father, who was very much a loner, William has always been popular and able to deal with the inevitable teasing that comes his way. The other boys were protective of him, particularly his few special friends. When he wrote to one of them after the accident, he asked them to be sure to lock the letters away so they didn't fall into 'enemy hands'.

If their parents questioned them, William's pals dismissed him with a shrug. 'He's good at games, loves football and plays in the under-11s team,' they'd say, but nothing more.

William was bright. His exam results were pinned in the corridor at Ludgrove along with those of the other boys; he was usually in the top half of his year. After Harry's arrival at the school, William was accused of flexing his muscles and was said to have held a fellow student's head down the loo and flushed it.

This punishment, William reckoned, was fair enough for someone telling tales, but despite his royal status the Prince was hauled before the headmaster and told not to repeat the feat.

Harry was popular too, but only with his contemporaries. The older boys found him just a bit too self-assured and cheeky. But the school has a reputation for smoothing the rough edges of its pupils and no doubt they encouraged Harry to assume a sense of humility.

Even with the hounds of speculation baying at their heels, Charles and Diana always tried to put on a united front when they were all together. They did what they could to shield their sons from the unpalatable and all-too-public enquiry into their marriage. In that the schools helped them.

The then headmaster of Ludgrove, Gerald Barber, and his wife Jane took great care of their young pupils, whoever they were. They were allowed to take a favourite teddy or cuddly toy to school, but radios were forbidden. There were no newspapers available at the school, and thus the boys were unable to read about the problems of William and Harry's parents.

Bad news has a way of filtering through. If the children didn't gossip, their parents certainly did, and Diana found herself wary of almost everyone. She would laugh to observe how some of the parents fawned around her, bowing and curtseying when she came into the dormitory – she called them affectionately the 'nods and the bobs'– but she didn't trust them.

Diana and Harry try out a jet-ski off St Tropez whilst holidaying on the French Riviera in July 1997

OPPOSITE PAGE: A month later, the Princes and their father are at the Falls of Muick, on the Balmoral estate

It was the constant backdrop of William and Harry's childhood and would leave an indelible impression on both of them. But from her own experiences Diana knew that however poor the relationship between the parents is, most children would prefer them to stay together. It was not to be. In December 1992 Prime Minister John Major announced in the House of Commons that the Prince and Princess of Wales were to separate.

William and Harry were at school. Charles and Diana went to see them to break the news. They went separately. It was the first taste of their future.

Their Christmas holiday that year was divided between their parents – with the royal side of their family taking precedence. The boys spent Christmas Day at Sandringham with their father who, anxious to reassert his parental position, had re-employed Mabel Anderson.

'It's just like old times,' said the Queen.

When they rejoined their mother she went one better than the dull flatlands of wintry Norfolk and whisked them off to the Caribbean. The difference in the holidays was symbolic of the different interests and contrasting priorities of their parents. But Diana insisted she would not be pushed into the background.

She was their mother and was determined to have her say in her sons' upbringing. If there was one inheritance she could give her children, Diana constantly reminded her friends, it was to allow them to grow up in an emotionally healthier and less deceptive environment than she did herself.

There is no doubt that Diana would have seen her sons as the most important legacy of her extraordinary life. She was the mother who taught them to care for others, who took them from their royal home to visit the terminally ill, the homeless and the sick; it was she who underlined the need for compassion. She taught them never to shout at anyone who could not answer back.

She introduced them to the 'modern' world and injected fun and excitement and thrills into their otherwise royally regulated lives.

Diana's 'boys', as she called them, were part of her very being. They were the reason for her existence and she was determined that whatever she might do in her own life it would come second to them. She went on to say that whatever her personal feelings were she would never taint her children's relationships with their father or anyone else in the royal family.

'I have no wish to upset what is essentially part of William's inheritance, whether he likes it or not,' Diana said.

The accident resulting in her death in Paris on 31 August 1997 robbed 15-year-old William, and Harry, 12, of a mother during some of their most difficult and formative years. But Prince Charles, who had largely remained in the background of their childhood, stood up and took over, at once becoming the father he had always tried to be.

For the rest of their lives William and Harry will have to contend with the controversy and scandal that is part of their mother's legacy. They are the custodians of her memory and if necessary will publically defend their mother's good name time and time again. Diana gave the royal family a powerful shove down the path towards becoming a soap opera. William wants to apply the brakes.

As a young man Charles's career was mapped out for him, his friends vetted, his activities closely chaperoned. He hated it and, according to Diana, it stunted his emotional growth. She was determined it would not happen to her boys. Nor has it.

Princes William and Harry have cause to be thankful to their mother for many things, but especially for refusing to allow the canopy of royal protocol to smother them.

William and Harry watch as their
mother's coffin is taken into
Westminster Abbey for her funeral

OPPOSITE PAGE: The brave Princes
walk with the Duke of Edinburgh, Earl
Spencer and their father to the abbey

Eugenie and Beatrice give their father an eve-of-birthday kiss during a skiing holiday in Verbier, February 2001

Beatrice & Eugenie

THE DUCHESS OF YORK once confided to me that she hated pregnancy: she didn't want to breastfeed; she just wasn't the 'mumsy' type. As with many women, the arrival of children changed her attitude. She became deeply attached to her daughters. And the end of her marriage to the Queen's favourite son drew her even closer to them.

'They are the only thing in my life that I know is one hundred per cent safe, loving and wonderful. They are my world,' she said, as she contemplated life without a husband.

In a real sense, Sarah was always a single parent. Andrew, as a serving officer in the Royal Navy, was away from home for months at a time and in 1990 only managed to spend 42 days with his family.

When their first child was born, the Prince's ship was in the Far East. He flew back from Singapore the day before the birth; two weeks later he was back with his ship. For the birth of their second child just over a year later he got there just in time, though Sarah wasn't sure if he would make it at all until he actually arrived.

'I don't like it,' the Duke of York said, 'but you have to take it otherwise the Navy wouldn't exist.' 'Never marry a sailor,' Sarah advised with feeling when their marriage broke up.

'Never marry a member of the royal family,' she might have added. Adapting to the disciplines and restrictions of royal life proved to be beyond her. Being married to someone whose own royal upbringing made him insensitive to those problems eventually proved intolerable.

On the early crest of what had been a genuine love affair – and despite Sarah's initial reservations about motherhood – the Duke and his Duchess approached parenthood with youthful enthusiasm.

They wanted lots of children, they declared, and when a 6lb 12oz girl was born on the numerically symmetrical date of 8.8.88 their marriage appeared to be settled on bedrock.

So it was, for a time. They had a large home; they employed a first-rate nanny named Alison Wardley, who had been a star pupil at the elite Princess Christian College in Manchester; they had a sizable staff to ensure their lives ran smoothly. But in this marriage appearances proved to be rather deceptive.

On an official visit to California, Sarah endeared herself to Americans with her cheery style ('I'll see you later,' she called back to a man in the crowd, who shouted 'I love you' at her), yet in Britain she attracted a barrage of prissy-lipped criticism from people who said that she wasn't behaving in the correct 'royal' way.

Then the death of the Queen's former equerry, Major Hugh Lindsay, in an avalanche at Klosters in March 1988 greatly upset the pregnant Duchess, who was part of the skiing party but had stayed behind in her chalet that fatal afternoon.

Next her 'darling Dads' – her paternal anchor since her mother had left home when Sarah was 13 – was discovered patronising a West End massage parlour. And as if that were not enough, she had to contend with a continuous barrage of criticism while her husband was away at sea.

The birth of Beatrice brought some respite. Two hundred cameramen waited for five days outside London's Portland Hospital for the first picture of the child, who was delivered by Mr Anthony Kenney. When Sarah and her princess finally made their appearance, it was estimated that 600 pictures were taken in the first second.

The public, as it does, applauded the newest member of the royal family. The praise would quickly die away again.

The Yorks went straight from the hospital to Balmoral, where Sarah introduced the Queen to 'Baby Yorklet' who, more formally, was fifth in line to the throne. Within a few days, however, Andrew was back at sea. He was reluctant to leave, and Sarah was reluctant to see him go, clinging to him up to the last moment and complaining that she felt like a single mother.

'He was never there for me when I needed him,' she later confided. 'And I didn't think I'd need him so much.'

Six weeks later the Duchess of York flew to Sydney to join him for a naval review to celebrate Australia's bicentennial. Beatrice was left behind in the care of her nanny. 'When would we have seen her?' Andrew said, defending their decision to leave her behind.

'Beatrice is much better off at home where things are stable, there is a routine and no constant upping and changing or haring around the countryside.'

It has been the fate of most royal children to be parted from their parents for long periods of time. George VI had left the Queen and the Queen had left Prince Charles at an early age. But there was an undercurrent of public hostility towards Sarah. It was her turn to become what Princess Michael of Kent called 'bad royal', and her decision to leave her child cast her in that role.

That Beatrice was in the attentive care of a team headed by Alison Wardley and helped by Mabel Anderson, who came out of retirement to care for her favourite royal baby's baby, was noted – and ignored. What had been acceptable in previous generations was not acceptable now and the decision to leave Beatrice behind provoked severe and enduring criticism.

'I thought it was more important to be with my husband,' Sarah said. 'It was his turn and I think that was the right thing to have done. I'm old-fashioned, but he comes first.'

Andrew's only advice to his wife was to ignore the criticism. It was a sad portent for the future.

Beatrice was named after Queen Victoria's ninth and final child, who is commemorated by a cairn on the Balmoral hillside that Sarah had often walked past. She was baptised four days before Christmas 1988.

By tradition, royal christenings were held in the Music Room at Buckingham Palace, but Andrew and Sarah insisted on holding the ceremony in the Chapel Royal at St James's Palace.

LEFT: The Duchess of York with Princess Beatrice at the Royal Windsor Horse Show in May 1990

OPPOSITE PAGE: Andrew and Sarah with their two-week-old daughter at Balmoral in a photograph taken by the Duke himself

The Yorks' firstborn was christened at the Chapel Royal, St James's Palace, on 20 December 1988

The Fergusons, including Sarah's grandmothers, Doreen Wright and Lady Elmhirst, along with most of the immediate royal family, crammed into the chapel, which was decorated with gold and white flowers to celebrate the baptism of the Queen's fifth grandchild, Princess Beatrice Elizabeth Mary of York. Eighteen-week-old Beatrice was kept amused by her father, who clutched an assortment of toys, a bottle and a rattle. The Archbishop of York, Dr John Habgood, performed the service at the silver-gilt lily font. The godparents were Jane, Duchess of Roxburghe, Viscount Linley, Peter Palumbo and two of Sarah's closest girlfriends, Carolyn Cotterell and Gabrielle Greenhall.

Once the ceremony was over, the day reverted to the usual pattern. The Queen led the guests back to Buckingham Palace for tea, neatly laid out on long tables in the Bow Room where liveried footmen served little éclairs, meringues, tiny doughnuts and sandwiches. There were four sets of royal children in attendance, all with their nannies. Princess Anne took it upon herself to preside over this regal crèche.

While guests drank tea or champagne, Andrew and his photographic mentor, Gene Nocon, hustled godparents and children in and out of an adjoining room for the official photographs. A photograph was taken of all the various children, including Sarah's half-sisters and half-brother, Eliza, Alice and Andrew.

'Eliza, being the youngest sat, next to Prince Harry and to make her smile they pretended Harry had a big spider and was going to put it up her leg.

'She didn't think it was funny at all!' recalled Sarah's stepmother, Sue Ferguson.

Fatherhood added a dimension to the Duke's hitherto regulated life. He took pleasure in bathing his baby daughter – a task he performed with military efficiency. As Sarah's sister, Jane Makim, recalled, 'He rolled up his sleeves, took off his

LEFT: The Yorks and Zara Phillips after Princess Eugenie's christening at Sandringham two days before Christmas 1990

OPPOSITE PAGE: Beatrice and her sister visit Chessington Zoo in Surrey with their mother in the autumn of 1991

watch and washed her thoroughly before he would let me play with her in the bath.'

The day-to-day responsibilities of bringing up Beatrice were left to his wife and the nanny, however. Sarah had a clear idea of how she wanted things done and she did not hesitate to tell Alison what she wanted. Alison, who had been taught never to monopolise a baby and always to allow the mother time alone with it, fell in with her employer's wishes.

'I was blessed with a super nanny who taught Beatrice everything, including how to swim almost as soon as she could walk,' Sarah acknowledged.

Because of Andrew's naval duties, special occasions like christenings and birthdays had to be fitted in around his schedule. Beatrice's first birthday party, for instance, was brought forward by a month and held on 8 July 1989 on the lawns of Castlewood House.

The theme that year was ragamuffin costumes for the children, dragons for the nannies. There was a jelly pit and a bouncy castle, and catering-size bottles of mustard and tomato ketchup for the children to spill over their hamburgers.

'And how many children are coming?' the Queen enquired of her daughter-in-law as she inspected the preparations. Sue Ferguson was about to tell her that over a hundred had been invited when Sarah got a warning kick in first and replied, 'Just a few friends, Ma'ama' (a blend of the formal 'ma'am' and the informal 'mama' she called the Queen by).

As it happened, the Queen enjoyed the hearty, boisterous fun and stayed for over an hour to watch the policemen organising races and eventually to present the prize for best-dressed ragamuffin. Royal protection officer Geoff Padgham's son won a prize. And from the other end of the social scale, so did one of Sarah's godchildren, Arabella Llewellyn, a great-niece of the Duke of Norfolk.

At the end of the lawn were outsize cardboard figures of Terry the butler in striped trousers and Alison the nanny in her Princess Christian uniform. Holes had been cut in their faces and everyone was invited to put their heads through and have crazy foam pies thrown at them (Andrew's idea).

'Ronald and I volunteered to do it first to get everyone going,' Sue Ferguson recalled. 'Prince Harry and Prince William thought it was wonderful being able to throw pies at us. All the adults had to take their turn, including Prince Charles, who was a good sport!'

Unknown to the guests Sarah was pregnant again. 'It was my secret and I was determined to keep it,' she said later. It was unplanned and not exactly unwanted. But she had not enjoyed her first confinement, and having just regained her figure – and her husband – was not over-enthusiastic about the idea of starting again so soon.

The struggle with what she called 'the system' – being continually told what she could and couldn't say or do – was starting to take its toll and her marriage was suffering.

Eugenie joins Beatrice at Upton House school in Windsor for the first time, 15 October 1992

OPPOSITE PAGE:
Princess Beatrice enjoys the school's sports day in June 1993

'Weekends were the worst,' she said. 'Andrew was tired and had the responsibilities of being a prince, not just a serving officer or husband. He had three jobs to do and I don't think anyone realised what a strain it was.'

On 23 March 1990, Sarah entered the Portland Hospital. She hoped to have the baby induced the following day, but it was found to be in the breech position: its feet were facing down and its head had not engaged. Again Mr Kenney was in charge, but he was unable to turn it as he had hoped. An emergency Caesarean operation was necessary. Andrew only just arrived in time, having driven from Plymouth where his frigate HMS *Cambeltown* was docked.

The baby, a girl weighing 7lb 1½oz, was born at 7.58pm. After the shock of the operation, Sarah, wrapped in the euphoria of the new baby, welcomed a string of visitors headed by the Queen, the Princess of Wales and Sarah's sister, Jane, who had flown over from Australia.

A week later her husband drove her home – and straight into another problem. Without telling her, Andrew had arranged for Gene Nocon to take official photographs of the family. Nocon's lights were already set up and he was waiting for them when they walked through the door with the baby.

The Duke wanted Nocon to have the pictures for exclusive use in one magazine but Sarah refused and insisted they go on general release. It was not their first disagreement, nor would it be their last. The photos attracted another wave of criticism.

It was further evidence, to Sarah at least, that her husband failed to comprehend the problems she faced. Again he returned to his naval duties. Again she was left to deal with the problems on her own. But now she also had to cope with two young children.

The name Beatrice had been inspired by a heap of stones at Balmoral. Princess Eugenie Victoria Helena was named after a portrait that hung at Windsor Castle.

'I liked the name at the bottom of the picture, Empress Eugenie,' Sarah explained. There is another Eugenie picture at Windsor. It is of Queen Victoria's granddaughter, Princess Victoria Eugenie of Battenberg, who later became Queen of Spain.

Sarah said: 'When I told the Queen I was going to

call the baby Eugenie she said she remembered Aunt Ena, as she called her, who had strawberry blonde hair tied up in a bun.' The Queen was referring to the second picture.

Eugenie – pronounced, according to Sarah, 'U-jean-ee', or, according to her sister, Jane, 'Me Tarzan, you Janie' – was christened on 23 December 1990 in the little church of St Mary Magdalene on the Sandringham estate. The baptism was performed during the regular Sunday service, with estate workers singing Christmas carols alongside the royal family.

'We all sang our hearts out,' Diana said afterwards.

The godparents were Andrew's cousin James Ogilvy, Royal Navy captain Alistair Ross, who was away on duty, Susan Ferguson and two of Sarah's 'three best friends', Lulu Blacker and Jules Dodd-Noble.

Sue Ferguson recalled the day. They drove up to Norfolk with Esme Tudor, Sarah's maternity nurse, 'and arrived so early we had to sit in a lay-by. We had been told to go to the Vicar of Sandringham's house, where we were met by Ronald's cousin, Sir Robert Fellowes [the Queen's Private Secretary], who was wearing an old tweed suit.'

After a cup of coffee with the vicar and Peter Nott, the Bishop of Norwich, they were taken in by the back entrance of the church. The godparents sat in the front pew, leaving the choir stalls free for the Queen and her family.

The church was a riot of festive colour, the stalls decked with chrysanthemums and holly. Two Christmas trees flanked the altar.

The congregation rose as Her Majesty and fourteen members of her family, including ten of the first eleven in line to the throne, filed in (Prince Charles was in the Persian Gulf on an official visit). Andrew and Sarah came in last carrying Princess Eugenie, sixth in line to the throne, with Beatrice running along in front.

'When she saw Eliza she ran to her pew and insisted on sitting next to her,' Sue said. 'Eugenie looked unwell. She had a high flush and Sarah told me she had a temperature and an ear infection. She was very grizzly.'

Forced into a tight, itchy christening robe designed for a baby younger than Eugenie's robust nine months, she was hot, tired and uncomfortable. She squirmed and wriggled throughout the long service and when the bishop finally took her from her mother and sprinkled holy water on her fevered brow she started to scream.

BWLOW: The Yorks, in public together for the first time since the divorce, and their daughters attend a charity event at Wentworth Golf Club in August 1996

OPPOSITE PAGE: The girls on a skiing holiday in Klosters, Switzerland, in January 1995 with their cousins William and Harry

Back at Sandringham House glasses of champagne greeted the churchgoers, who had been warned by Fellowes that a television crew would be present.

'The children loved it,' Sue recalled. 'They were interviewed and asked what they wanted for Christmas. Prince Andrew said he would like a golf bag!'

Elsewhere, Cockney photographer Terry O'Neill was trying to organise the official photographs. As usual, Prince Philip was tetchy and impatient.

'Haven't you taken enough?' he kept saying. 'I can't believe anyone can take so long just to take a few boring photographs.' The Queen smiled. O'Neill, the ultimate professional, ignored Philip's rudeness and kept snapping. The real problem was Eugenie's red blotchy face, made worse by her tears.

Round tables of eight had been arranged to accommodate the luncheon party. Each member of the family hosted a table.

The Duke of Edinburgh entertained the godparents; the Princess of Wales entertained the children. Sarah asked the Queen if the nannies and Terry O'Neill could join the royal gathering.

The Queen found it difficult to refuse her lively daughter-in-law and an extra table was hastily set up.

And so it was that a relief nanny, who had arrived from Australia only the previous day, found herself sitting down to lunch with the Queen of England.

Afterwards, Diana took all the children into another room to watch a film. Everyone else retired to the drawing room for coffee, where the Queen and Prince Philip discussed the merits of the menu.

When the party eventually broke up some of the guests paused to sit on the scales in the front hall. It is a Sandringham tradition for guests to weigh themselves when they arrive and again when they leave to see how much they have notched up. Beside the scales are neatly-stacked piles of dog towels. They also form part of the Sandringham ritual.

'When we left,' Sue Ferguson recalled, 'Sarah and Andrew stood at the door and waved the dog towels. It was rather strange but obviously a Sandringham tradition.'

Such events provide the set pieces of royal life. Contrary to impressions, however, the royal family does not live in an up-market commune, one on top of the other, in everyday contact with each other. Sarah had her own home to run where she was free to bring up her children in her own way. She respected the old-fashioned virtues of manners and discipline but also embraced the more modern approach of keeping her children around her and allowing them to be part of her life.

'I was frightfully strict about manners,' Sarah's mother, Susie Barrantes recalled. 'My own mother was brought up strictly and correctly and I think it rubs off on you.'

When the girls asked for pet rabbits they were given them, but when they failed to look after them the bunnies were taken away again. And each evening, after they had had their tea,

they were taught to put their hands together in prayer to thank God for their food.

Sarah, without the steadying influence of a husband to call on, was not always as strict as she might have been and she particularly dreaded taking them aboard the Royal Yacht *Britannia*, where they had a tendency to run riot, Eugenie especially. Beatrice was more placid and had shown no signs of jealousy when her sister was born, regarding her not as competition but as her own 'dolly'.

Beatrice was the more girly of the two. She was passionate about anything pink, loved having her hair tied with ribbons and was very attached to the Disney cartoon character, the Little Mermaid. She had a Little Mermaid swimsuit, lots of pink pyjamas and nighties, and her bedroom at the rented home in Wentworth her mother moved into after she parted from Andrew was decorated with pink Nina Campbell wallpaper.

Eugenie, on the other hand, was very independent and adventurous, though in matters athletic each was as good as the other. They learned to ride on a pony called Smokey who had also been used by Peter and Zara Phillips and then princes William and Harry.

When it was her turn to sit in the saddle, Eugenie, aged two, did so with a determined disregard for personal safety. 'Boojie', as her parents call Eugenie, set her jaw and kicked away with her little heels. Sarah jokingly called her 'my monster'.

Andrew, away so much of the time, had little direct influence on the early development of his daughters, although he did make the effort to read to them at bedtime when he was at home. His interest in his children was only patchy, however, and it was Sarah's ideas that prevailed.

'I don't believe in sending them to school too early,' she said. 'I'm against boarding school, but obviously I'll be under a bit of pressure about that. I think home life is very important. I've got two lovely girls and what's the point of sending them to school for months on end? I don't believe it's right. I think it's important to see them and teach them about life through your eyes as well.

LEFT: The Duchess of York tidies her younger daughter's hair at a Children in Crisis pro-celebrity golf tournament in July 1998

OPPOSITE PAGE: Eugenie joins her paternal grandparents on the Buckingham Palace balcony after the 1998 Birthday Parade

'I like to take them away with me to see new cultures and learn. The more they travel the more they can grow and learn about people in new parts of the world. It stimulates the imagination.

'I won't let them get spoiled. Beatrice might be a little precocious, but that's the run of children that age. She's got her own character and I'm not going to squash it. She goes everywhere with me when it is possible to take her and I speak to her on a one-to-one basis. I don't talk down to her. She's my friend and we talk about everything.'

'She's very sensible and consistent with the children,' Sarah's stepmother observed. 'She doesn't get hysterical and she doesn't pamper them.'

When Beatrice crashed her tricycle into a table in the hallway and spilt the wax of a burning candle over herself, Sarah calmly took her in her arms and said, 'It doesn't hurt, it doesn't hurt. Be brave, it's all over and there is no need to cry any more,' while Andrew wiped the grease off with a towel.

'It was the right way of dealing with it,' said Sue Ferguson, who witnessed the incident. 'Sarah has the right attitude when dramas happen.'

When Sarah and Andrew separated in 1992, she explained to Beatrice, then three and a half, that they would no longer be living with Papa but they would see him just as much – and maybe more.

'Who is looking after Papa?' Beatrice enquired. 'Doesn't he miss us?'

Sarah did her best to protect her daughters from the trauma of the parting. She was helped in that by their young age, and she assured Beatrice that Papa was all right. It was not always easy, though.

'For young children in particular, exclusion from the warmth and safety of a home and family seems a horrendous exile and children worry about the absent parent,' said child psychologist Penelope Leach.

Beatrice sometimes called out: 'I want my Papa'.

She did just that on the day Sarah left Balmoral after the publication of embarassing photographs taken in the south of France.

With the Duchess about to drive away from the castle, Beatrice started shouting, 'I don't want to go. I want to stay here with Papa.' Sarah remembered her heart sinking into her shoes.

It was the very last thing she wanted to happen at that moment. But she remained calm. 'Don't worry – Papa's going to work soon,' she told her daughter.

Beatrice also wanted her mother, of course. She was at what Leach called the 'clinging' stage, and when the girls went to see Andrew Sarah always had to go too.

Again according to Leach, children of that young age 'usually refuse to believe in the fact or the permanency of the separation'. On that score, however, Sarah was adamant. No entreaties by the Queen could persuade her to reconsider her marital situation.

'I can't live a lie,' she explained. 'He is my friend. I love him. But I can't go back.' The pressures of being a member of the royal family had finally proved too much for her.

She was equally single-minded, though, in her determination to stay on friendly terms with Andrew, who remained remarkably supportive towards her throughout the tribulations of the separation, even when those intimate photographs of Sarah on holiday in the south of France with her financial advisor John Bryan were published.

For a long time the Duke of York hoped for a reconciliation. He kept the marital home just as she had left it. On his side of the bed, piled on a bedside table, were all his books, papers and personal things. On her side, nothing.

Eventually Andrew was forced to admit Sarah was not coming back. But he refused ever to believe she had had an affair and still holds out hope to this day that they could be a family again, which is possible once Sarah's main antagonist, the Duke of Edinburgh, is no longer around to prevent it.

There were plenty of dramas in Sarah's life, but whatever personal turmoil she experienced she remained composed in front of her children.

In spite of their nomadic childhood – the girls were shunted around a string of rented houses when their parents split up before they finally settled at Royal Lodge with their father – they are well adjusted and caring.

LEFT: Princess Beatrice, accompanied by her parents, arrives for her first day at St George's School in Ascot, 6 September 2000

OPPOSITE PAGE: She and Prince William at St George's Chapel in June 1999 after the wedding of Prince Edward to Sophie Rhys-Jones

The Duchess stopped using them as her 'passport' and it is to her great credit that they both have such a well-developed philanthropic side and by using their own early experiences, support several different charitable causes.

When she was 12 Eugenie had to undergo an eight-hour operation for scoliosis (curvature of the spine) at the Royal National Orthopaedic Hospital and have metal rods and screws inserted in her spine to prevent her from ending up in a wheelchair. Beatrice suffered from dyslexia, which she made public knowledge to help others with that condition.

After the divorce Sarah never stood in the way of the girls spending every Christmas and some of their holidays with the Queen at Sandringham and Balmoral.

The monarch has always had a soft spot for Sarah and, despite Prince Philip's misgivings, allowed her to throw a lavish 18th birthday party at Windsor Castle for Beatrice. Like her first birthday party, it was beautifully arranged but totally over the top.

Beatrice, educated at Coworth Park School, Windsor and later at St George's Ascot, where she was head girl (Eugenie

went to Marlborough College), is considerably more intellectual than either her father or mother. She has a 2:1 degree (BA) in history and the history of ideas from Goldsmiths College and feels it is her duty to put something back into what she sees as her world of royal privilege.

She has seen it all from ground level, having lived alongside her mother's disasters and dramas when it might have been better for her to have been spared the adversity.

'I love being who I am,' Princess Beatrice says, and although the Prince of Wales appears not to require the help of her or Eugenie in his future 'slimmed-down monarchy', they both could be of enormous benefit.

Eugenie, who was only two when her parents separated, has, according to her father, a maverick streak and is the livelier of the two girls. She too has experienced a lot of emotion in her short life. Eugenie was just seven and Beatrice nine when Diana, Princess of Wales died.

The sudden death of 'Auntie Duch', as they called Diana, was a terrible shock – as was the death of their grandmother Susie Barrantes, also in a car crash – but it was the terminal cancer of their grandfather, Ronald Ferguson, which affected them most.

His bravery and the slow progression of his illness allowed them to experience first-hand the preciousness of life and the meaning of dignity in death. These were indeed very useful lessons for young princesses.

Despite their divorce, Andrew and Sarah have remained the greatest of friends and spend an inordinate amount of time together, with Sarah enjoying the benefit of a suite of rooms at Royal Lodge as her home.

Beatrice and Eugenie's future is more certain than that of their mother and the Duke of York is understandably keen that they have some sort of official royal role. They have certainly proved themselves to be amongst the Queen's favourite grandchildren.

'She is one of the most amazing women ever,' Princess Eugenie has said of her royal grandmother. 'She is also very funny. You can tell when she is happy, having all her family round at Christmas and watching them all laugh and have so much fun on Christmas Day. It just makes her very happy.'

The 'magical two daughters', as Sarah describes Beatrice and Eugenie, look set to make a success of their lives whatever path they choose to take.

RIGHT: The similarly-dressed siblings attend a service of thanksgiving at Windsor Castle on 10 June 2001 to mark the Duke of Edinburgh's 80th birthday

OPPOSITE PAGE: Eugenie's first day at St George's School, 6 September 2001

The Earl and Countess of Wessex leave Frimley Park Hospital with their baby daughter, 23 November 2003

Louise & James

ALTHOUGH HE WAS born into the most public family in the world, Prince Edward grew up to be determinedly egalitarian. Of all the Queen's children he was most keenly aware of his position and attendant privileges and, rather like Prince Harry today, was bothered by what he saw as the burden of his royal birth.

The Royal Marines and later the theatre widened Edward's perspective, but he was still not comfortable perched on the pedestal of his royal status. He decided that when and if he married and started a family, his wife-to-be would have to be totally familiar with the palace system and know exactly what she was letting herself in for.

When Edward met and fell in love with Sophie Rhys-Jones in 1993, he persuaded the Queen that she should be allowed to live in his suite of rooms at Buckingham Palace before he even considered proposing marriage.

It was an eminently sensible way of familiarising 27-year-old Sophie with a family of enormous complexity. She was given her own pass, which allowed her to come and go as she pleased, and she came to know the senior courtiers of the Royal Household who had allegedly made Diana's – and later

Fergie's – lives so difficult. A prolonged courtship helped: they met in September 1993 when Sophie was working in public relations and married in June 1999. Sophie maintains she is still learning about how the royal family works.

On their wedding day, the Queen announced that Edward would eventually be Duke of Edinburgh, but until such time would be known as Earl of Wessex with the subsidiary title Viscount Severn, the latter reflecting his bride's Welsh roots. Sophie became Countess of Wessex at the ceremony in St George's Chapel, Windsor Castle.

The Queen gave the couple the use of Bagshot Park in Surrey. Sophie and Edward renovated the vast Victorian mansion, set in parkland and gardens, turning it into an ideal place to bring up the family they so looked forward to having.

Getting pregnant and staying pregnant was to become a real problem for Sophie. In December 2001 she was rushed to King Edward VII Hospital in central London, under the auspices of the Queen's obstetrician-gynaecologist, Marcus Setchell, suffering from a potentially life-threatening ectopic pregnancy. Six weeks pregnant at the time, Sophie collapsed and needed an emergency operation.

The Countess lost so much blood she had to stay in hospital for four days. It would be another two years before IVF treatment enabled her to fall pregnant again.

In November 2003 – one month before the baby was due – Sophie was at home watching television when she began to suffer from sharp abdominal pains. Prince Edward was 6,000 miles away in Mauritius on an official visit, so she telephoned her GP, Dr Jonathan Holliday. Rushing to her side, he diagnosed the pains as a possible sudden placental abruption, a condition where the placenta ruptures without warning from the lining of the womb.

The condition – which deprives the baby of oxygenated blood – can lead to brain damage or, in some cases, can even be fatal. Realising this, the doctor requested an ambulance to take Sophie to the nearest hospital. It was 9.59pm.

At 10.20pm an anxious Dr Holliday was still waiting for the ambulance when he realised there had been a mix up. A second ambulance answered the emergency call and drove to Bagshot Park.

The Countess was put on a stretcher and, with sirens blaring, was driven to nearby Frimley Park Hospital. It was now 11pm. Within 32 minutes Sophie had given birth to a 4lb 9oz girl, delivered by Caesarean section. Marcus Setchell was present for the operation carried out by surgeon Sukhpal Singh with gynaecologist Anne Deans and midwife Adrienne Prince.

The infant was immediately transferred to the neo-natal unit at St George's Hospital in Tooting, southwest London, for specialist treatment, leaving heavily-sedated Sophie behind.

The baby was accompanied by a royalty protection officer as well as her own medical team.

Prince Edward, attending a reception in Mauritius, was told of the drama and dashed to the airport to catch the first flight out – which was to Paris. He faced an agonising eight-hour flight until he landed in the French capital and was transferred to a waiting RAF jet to Farnborough, a ten-minute drive from the hospital. As soon as he arrived he rushed to Sophie's side and then on to St George's to see his new daughter.

In the days that followed Edward did his best to comfort his wife, taking pictures and videos of the baby to show her. After six days the child was strong enough to be taken back to Frimley Park Hospital. An emotional Prince told reporters how wonderful it was to be a family together for the first time and how grateful he was for everyone's help and support.

BELOW: Lady Louise and her mother watch the State Opening of Parliament procession from a window at Buckingham Palace in November 2007

OPPOSITE PAGE: Edward and his daughter disembark from *Hebridean Princess* in July 2006 after a family holiday to belatedly mark the Queen's 80th birthday

After 11 days in Frimley Park, the Countess of Wessex was allowed home, without the baby. Although Sophie looked well, she had almost lost her life due to the confusion and subsequent late arrival of the ambulance at Bagshot Park.

Buckingham Palace announced that the baby would be called Lady Louise Alice Elizabeth Mary Mountbatten-Windsor. Louise was the name of Edward's paternal great-great-grandmother; Alice was the name of his paternal grandmother, Princess Alice of Greece, and Elizabeth was the name of both the Queen and the Queen Mother. Mary was the name of Sophie's mother and Edward's great-grandmother, Queen Mary.

Lady Louise was baptised on 24 April 2004 in the private chapel at Windsor Castle, where Edward had been christened 30 years earlier.

There were two close family members amongst their godparents – Edward's cousin and childhood companion, Lady Sarah Chatto, and Lord Ivar Mountbatten. The others were Lady Alexander Etherington, only daughter of the Duke of Fife; Francesca Schwarzenbach, a former Miss Australia and the wife of a Swiss billionaire, Urs Schwarzenbach; and Edward's Cambridge University contemporary, Rupert Elliott.

Louise behaved impeccably and slept through most of the ceremony.

It had been a very difficult time for Edward and Sophie, and although Louise appeared to be healthy, they discovered she was suffering from extropia, a condition where one eye turns outwards. A combination of surgery and physiotherapy is said to cure this condition over time.

Louise had her first operation at the age of three and seems relaxed and unbothered by her condition, which is improving as therapy technology moves forward.

Sophie was happy to have a child at last. She later admitted that her memories of seeing her daughter for the first time after the birth were a 'blur'.

She also confessed that she was terrified when she saw the tiny baby fighting for her life in an incubator.

'It's quite frightening when you can't see them for the wires,' she recalled. Sophie had trouble finding clothes petite enough to fit Louise when she first came home, as even the smallest outfits proved to be too big for her.

In July 2007, Buckingham Palace announced that the Wessexes were expecting their second child.

Sophie was taking no chances with this pregnancy and although she continued with royal duties, on the advice of Marcus Setchell she did scale them back.

On 17 December she gave birth to a 6lb 2oz boy by Caesarean section in a private suite at Frimley Park. This time Prince Edward was present for the birth and admitted, 'it was a lot calmer than last time'.

Talking to reporters, Edward told them his wife was doing well and that their son 'was like most babies, rather small, very cute and very cuddly'.

LEFT: The Wessexes and Louise on the balcony of Buckingham Palace after the Queen's Birthday Parade in June 2009

OPPOSITE PAGE: One month earlier, the entire family enjoy all the fun of the fair at the Royal Windsor Horse Show

When asked if they had chosen any names the Prince said cautiously that since they had opted not to know the sex of the baby, they were not sure. They must have had some ideas, however, as only two days later it was announced the infant was to be named James Alexander Philip Theo, with his father's subsidiary title, Viscount Severn. They both liked the names James and Alexander, and had chosen Philip as a tribute to Prince Philip and Theo after Sophie's grandfather.

As grandchildren of a monarch through the male line, the Wessex children are entitled to be known as HRH Princess Louise and HRH Prince James. When Edward and Sophie married, however, the Queen announced that any children would be styled as those of an earl, hence Lady Louise Mountbatten-Windsor and Viscount Severn.

The Queen couldn't wait for Edward and Sophie to bring her eighth grandchild up to Sandringham to enjoy the Christmas celebrations, which they duly did. It made sense for them to be there as they could then allow their own small staff to have Christmas off. James was just a week old and Sophie was recovering from the operation, but Sandringham is used to babies and every amenity was laid on so she would be as comfortable as possible.

The Queen is extremely fond of Sophie and was insistent she should take it easy after James's birth and make time to enjoy her young family. But in January 2008 the Wessexes had another scare when little James suffered an allergic reaction and was rushed into London's Great Ormond Street Hospital for treatment. Sophie was so worried that she and Edward stayed overnight with the baby in the hospital.

On 19 April 2008 James was christened in the private chapel at Windsor Castle with the Queen, Prince Philip and Sophie's father, Christopher Rhys-Jones, in attendance. Princess Anne and Prince Andrew were also there, as was little Louise, who insisted on kissing and trying to cuddle her little brother. James wore a replica of the satin and Honiton lace royal gown his sister had worn at her christening.

The original gown made in 1841 was considered just too fragile and in order to preserve it, the Queen had asked her personal assistant Angela Kelly to have an exact copy made.

BELOW: Bridesmaid Louise and her cousin Harry ride in an open carriage to Buckingham Palace after William and Kate's wedding, 29 April 2011

OPPOSITE PAGE: At the 2011 Royal Windsor Horse Show the Queen playfully lifts up Louise's cap to find her youngest granddaughter underneath

The Right Reverend David Conner, Dean of Windsor, conducted the service and the godparents were mostly old friends: historian Alistair Bruce, now Sky Television's ceremonial commentator; Duncan Bullivant, founder of a security protection business, who has known Prince Edward since their schooldays; Denise Poulton, Sophie's friend and a trustee of the Wessex Trust; and American-born Jeanye Irwin, who once shared a flat with Sophie. Tom Hill, another old friend, completed the group.

Edward has always loved Windsor and considered it his home. He chose to live at nearby Bagshot Park and, when his children were old enough to go to school, he and Sophie picked St George's, in the shadow of Windsor Castle. Founded in the 14th century, the school has provided choristers for the chapel at Windsor since 1352.

Children don't have to be musical to be admitted and Lady Louise was amongst the 140 pre-prep pupils who start as early as three years old. She can remain at the school until she is 13, which is most convenient as the sports fields are actually in the Queen's 'back garden', Home Park (Private).

Neither James nor Louise has protection officers with them in the classroom, as Prince Edward did, and Sophie drives herself when she takes the children to school. Their life is simple by royal standards and although Bagshot Park is a large house it is run efficiently with a housekeeper, a gardener and a butler-cum-factotum, who does everything from answering the telephone to serving at mealtimes.

The Countess would prefer not to have to employ the services of a nanny but the couple's royal workload is such that they must. Three days a week Sophie is out on official duties and a further two are spent preparing for them, including meeting with representatives from the organisations with which she is involved.

She makes a point of being home after school if she possibly can and devotes the rest of her day to the children. Louise and James are pony mad – much to their grandmother's delight – and the Queen keeps two ponies for them in the Royal Mews at Windsor.

Last year Louise fell off hers whilst riding in the park and broke her left arm. Ever cautious after her daughter's difficult entry into the world, Sophie cancelled an official visit to Manchester and took Louise to hospital, where her arm was put in a cast. It did not deter the eight-year-old and she was back in the saddle as soon as she was allowed to be.

LEFT: The Countess of Wessex and Lady Louise Mountbatten-Windsor attend a reception at Guildhall after the Diamond Jubilee thanksgiving service, 5 June 2012

OPPOSITE PAGE: Sophie takes flag-waving Louise and James to an Olympic equestrian dressage grand prix in Greenwich Park, August 2012

Sophie, not nearly as accomplished a rider as her husband, has suffered many falls and two days before Prince William's wedding broke a couple of ribs. However much pain she was in nothing would have made her miss Louise's debut as a royal bridesmaid.

Louise was so excited when she was told she had been chosen and both Sophie and Edward were thrilled to see how happy it made her. She proudly waved to the crowd as she drove from Westminster Abbey to Buckingham Palace in an open carriage sitting next to Prince Harry.

From the age of six Louise became more visible at royal events, joining in the Diamond Jubilee service of thanksgiving at St Paul's Cathedral and the Queen's Birthday Parade.

The years of shielding their children from the press are not over, but Sophie and Edward are conscious that the time they will be able to spend with their paternal grandparents is limited.

The Earl and Countess want their children to attend as many family events as possible and spend weekends and holidays around the Queen and Prince Philip at Windsor and Balmoral. They have bonded with their grandmother and love doing 'horsey' things with her.

According to the Hon. Margaret Rhodes, the Queen's cousin, Prince Philip is also surprisingly good with young children and, like many grandparents, loves having them around.

'I remember him dandling one of the Wessex babies on his knee at Balmoral,' she said. 'It is quite in variance to his image, but he genuinely loves his grandchildren.'

RIGHT: James, Viscount Severn has a ride on a rocking horse at the 2013 Royal Windsor Horse Show

OPPOSITE PAGE: The following month he attended the Queen's Birthday Parade for the first time

Peter and Autumn Phillips with Savannah and Isla at Badminton Horse Trials in Gloucestershire, May 2013

Savannah & Isla

WHEN PETER PHILLIPS met Canadian beauty Autumn Kelly at the Montreal Grand Prix in June 2003 she had no idea who he was. Having been raised on the West Island region of Montreal there was no reason for her to have heard of him or the Phillips family. Six weeks later, after visiting Peter in Oxford for a long weekend, she still had no idea.

It was only when watching television with her mother and seeing Peter on screen standing next to Prince William that she realised who he was. She admitted later she felt a bit of a fool, but Peter Phillips has always valued his privacy.

Princess Anne and Captain Mark Phillips refused titles for Peter and his sister, Zara, first grandchildren of the Queen and the Duke of Edinburgh. 'We will be forever indebted to our parents for what they did for us,' Peter explains, 'because they have allowed us to have a normal life.

'My father always made it clear I would have to work for a living and that handouts would not be forthcoming.'

Peter's work in sports sponsorship took him to Hong Kong, Edinburgh and back to London, where he currently works for the UK arm of an Australian sports and entertainment agency.

In the summer of 2007, 29-year-old Peter announced his engagement to Autumn Kelly, also 29. Renouncing her Roman Catholic faith, she converted to the Church of England, not only to keep Peter in the line of succession but because she wanted to be the same religion as any children they might have. Autumn was also aware that her future mother-in-law, the Princess Royal, is the daughter of the Supreme Governor of the Church of England.

Autumn's renunciation of her Catholic faith drew attention to the Act of Settlement's insistence that anyone in line to the throne who marries a Catholic must relinquish their place and prompted calls in both Canada and the United Kingdom for the respective governments to address the issue.

Confident as she was around Peter's family, Autumn wanted to do everything correctly and when she needed advice was given a guiding hand by Peter's cousin, Lady Sarah Chatto.

'Peter's grown up with protocol,' Autumn explained, 'and he just knows, but for somebody like me who has come from the outside it can be quite daunting.'

According to Autumn, it was the Princess Royal who helped her perfect a look for royal occasions that is smart, functional and pretty without spending a fortune on designer clothes, something Anne certainly does not do.

After Autumn and Peter's wedding at St George's Chapel, Windsor Castle, on 17 May 2008, followed by a reception at Frogmore House, the couple moved to Hong Kong. Peter continued to work for the sponsorship division of the Royal Bank of Scotland, where he was put in charge of the bank's motor-racing sponsorship interests in the Far East.

They led a comfortable life befitting Peter's employment, but he knew it wouldn't last forever and when the bank cut back on sponsorship the Phillipses returned to the UK. Autumn then worked for a management consultancy and looked after TV personality Sir Michael Parkinson. Once she became pregnant, however, she gradually reduced her work schedule so she could prepare for family life.

'I don't want to have a baby and hand it to someone else,' Autumn said. 'We don't really have nannies in Canada – well I'm sure some people do, but my family didn't. I like to raise my own children, though once they start school I'll have to find a job again.'

Savannah – the Queen's first great-grandchild – was born on 29 December 2010 at Gloucestershire Royal Hospital. At 8lb 8oz she was a big baby and Peter stayed at his wife's side throughout the labour and birth. As he is not a working member of the royal family he is not obliged to reveal any personal information about the child and he did not do so. The name of the baby, 12th in line to the throne at the time, was let slip during a service at the church of St Mary Magdalene at Sandringham the following Sunday. The Rector, the Reverend Jonathan Riviere, prayed for 'Peter and Autumn and their daughter Savannah'.

Afterwards, a well-wisher congratulated Princess Anne outside the church and said she imagined that baby Savannah would be spoilt.

'Not by me,' the Princess retorted.

After a private christening on 23 April 2011 at the Church of the Holy Cross in the village of Avening in Gloucestershire, attended by the Queen and the Duke of Edinburgh, the baby's full names were revealed to be Savannah Anne Kathleen Phillips.

The name Savannah was made popular in North America after a 1982 movie, *Savannah Smiles*, which is why Autumn chose the charming – but not traditionally royal – name. Anne was by way of a compliment to her paternal grandmother, and Kathleen after her own mother. Little Savannah has the advantage of having Canadian and British citizenship, which makes her the first Canadian citizen to be so close to the royal family.

Home for the Phillips family is a London apartment and a beautiful Cotswold farmhouse, Aston Farm on the Gatcombe estate. Autumn' s life has changed massively since she became a full-time mother and she relishes being able to live in the English countryside and devote herself to her children. Peter's work involves a lot of travelling, but he always tries to get home to see his wife and growing family even though it means commuting from Gloucestershire to the London office of SEL, an Australia-based sports and entertainment company, in Knightsbridge.

On 29 March 2012, Autumn gave birth to their second child, another girl, Isla Elizabeth, weighing 7lb 4oz. Isla, a name that reflects Peter's love of Scotland, was christened in the church of St Nicholas in Cherington, Gloucestershire, on 1 July.

Only 15 months separates the girls, both born on the 29th of the month, so Autumn has her work cut out. Grandmother Kathleen came from Canada to help, but although Princess Anne dotes on her two grandchildren, her busy royal schedule left her little time to be of much practical use.

Savannah Phillips, the Queen's first great-grandchild, sits on the grass while she enjoys an ice-cream

OPPOSITE PAGE: The proud parents take their firstborn to the 2011 Festival of British Eventing at Gatcombe Park

Peter is, however, very much a hands-on dad, as Captain Mark Phillips confirmed. 'Peter has proved to be a great father – much better than I was.'

'Peter was a very well-behaved little boy; he wasn't much trouble,' he added. 'He knew where the line was and he didn't cross it. I was never good with small children. But once Peter and Zara could walk and talk and be useful I could relate to them much more.'

An honest statement from a father. Not all men can interact with very young children and Mark Phillips obviously was one of them, although he loved a rough and tumble with them when they were older.

Savannah and Isla, as befitting their equine royal heritage, are growing up around horses, so it would be surprising if the two girls didn't show some sort of interest in riding.

At the age of only two, Savannah was given a pony by Auntie Zara and loved being hoisted on and off, although she was too little for much more.

'Zara was insistent on giving her a little Shetland pony,' Peter explained. 'Savannah loves riding him so it seems as if we've passed on the horse gene to the next generation.'

The Phillips children were on horseback as soon as they could sit still long enough, and Zara wanted to ensure that a pony was available for her brother's children to learn on, just as there was for her. The Queen enjoys seeing her grandchildren and great-grandchildren learn to ride, and both she and Prince Philip like having the little ones around.

'It's a natural thing for grandparents to eventually want to be great-grandparents and they love it,' says Peter. 'It's nice for them to have another batch of youngsters running around and coming to visit them.'

He realises the importance of his children seeing a little of what their great-grandparents do, whether they remember it or not.

'If you want a role model for someone who works hard, then my grandparents are it,' Peter concludes. It is something he will pass on to his family.

LEFT: Autumn Phillips and 13-month-old Isla take a walk in the spring sunshine in Gloucestershire

OPPOSITE PAGE: Two-and-a-half-year-old Savannah bears a distinct resemblance to her father at the same age

FOR 33 YEARS *Majesty* magazine has been bringing its readers all they need to know about the royal families of the world. Each issue contains knowledgeable features and beautiful photography, with news and views on the personalities, lifestyles, fashions and homes of royals past and present.

From the births of princes and princesses to fairy-tale royal weddings to jubilee celebrations, *Majesty* provides the full story. Intimate interviews with royalty and those who know them offer a unique insight into their privileged lives.

Majesty records all the important royal engagements and takes an in-depth look at the dramatic history of Britain's monarchs. Month by month it builds into a stunning and authoritative royal collection.

Acknowledgements

Special thanks are due to Darren Reeve, Annette Prosser and Sarah Hill for their invaluable assistance with the production of *A Century of Royal Children*.